ROBB

C000277378

My Liverpool life: The Rob Jones story

By Rob Jones

with

Paul Hassall

Kids Academy Publishing
Grimsditch House
Grimsditch Lane
Warrington
WA4 4ED

Published in 2012 by Kids Academy Publishing

A catalogue record of this book is available from the British library

ISBN 978-09574571-0-2

Printed in Great Britain by Carlton Print Management, Walton
Lodge, Hill Cliffe Road, Walton, Warrington. WA4 6NU

For Sue, Natalie, Amy and Declan

Acknowledgements

I would like to thank the following people for their help in the publication of this book:

Stephen Done, Getty Images and Liverpool Football Club for providing us with the relevant photographs of my playing days.

Stephen Astall at Liverpool FC, Cliff Butler at Manchester United, Ged Rea, Sheldon Xavier, Milesh Chudasama and my mum, Joan, my dad Pete and my other dad, Paul.

I would also like to express my appreciation to Ryan Giggs, Dario Gradi, Graeme Souness and Jamie Carragher for their kind words and anecdotes of their encounters with me.

Finally I would like to thank Macca and Robbie for providing the forewords to my story. It was a bit like picking your best man when it came to deciding which one I'd like to do it and in the end I wanted them both to have their say.

I hope you enjoy the read.

Rob Jones

CONTENTS

FOREWORD I

STEVE MCMANAMAN

As far as I'm concerned Rob Jones is the best right-back England *never* had.

He's also the finest player to have ever represented Liverpool Football Club - and not score a goal.

'Trigger' had to retire when he was the best right-back around so I think that it's only right that fans who maybe don't realise just how good he was, can understand the highs and lows he enjoyed as a professional footballer.

He's got a story to tell and I think it shows a different side to the game.

There have been a lot of tales about the triumphs and successes that footballers have enjoyed over the years but Rob's is one that focuses on how a great talent can fall victim to the tragedy of injury.

I remember him joining the club as one of Graeme Souness's first signings and being thrown into a debut at Manchester United. That's difficult in its own right but to then have to mark Ryan Giggs, who was the next big superstar at the time, was something else entirely. What Giggs has gone on to achieve in his career illustrates just how impressive that was.

Many, many players would have frozen on such a massive stage but Rob rose to the occasion. He kept Giggsy quiet and I think you could see, even at that point, that Liverpool had a real find on their hands.

Unless you have actually played in games of such intensity and fierce rivalry, I don't think you can truly comprehend how difficult it is to perform in a match of that magnitude.

So to do it on your debut, within days of arriving from an old fourth division club, speaks volumes for him.

We became great friends from the moment he arrived. We had a good relationship both on and off the pitch. The fact we had such a brilliant bond off the field undoubtedly helped when we linked up on it. He always seemed to give me the pass at the right time and also understood when the right moment was to go past me.

A lot of people ask me about playing for Real Madrid and the partnership I had with Michel Salgado down the right. He always wanted to give me the ball and then rampage forward.

That wasn't just on occasion. That was ALL of the time. That could be quite maddening.

As a wide midfielder you often receive the ball and look to pop it off straight away because your marker is too close. I couldn't really do that with Salgado but Rob instinctively knew when to overlap and when to hold his position.

He was great at reading a situation, always solid in defence and a fine attacker too. His pace meant he was a superb asset for the team and when he did get in behind the full-back his crossing ability was excellent.

He was your quintessential right-back and it's hard to identify anyone who played in that position who was better than him.

If it wasn't for Trigger's injury, I think he would have gone down in history as one of the greatest right-backs England has ever produced.

He should have been his country's first-choice for over a decade.

Some people would point to Gary Neville, a player who went on to be England's most-capped right-back ever with 85 appearances to his name. I agree, there's no doubt Gary achieved great things in the game. But at the time Trigger was a better footballer, without a shadow of a doubt.

He was stronger going forward and was certainly quicker. I think he was a better player on the ball with more of an ability to take people on too.

It was a real tragedy that his career was cut short at the age of 27. But if you chat to Rob, he is always keen to talk about the positives.

Yes, he had some bad times but he also got to live the dream of playing for the club he supported as a kid. It's important to remember that he still played 243 games for one of the biggest clubs in the world. I know he is still held in high esteem by the Liverpool supporters.

He's always asked about his inability to score a goal and looking back I just can't understand how he didn't manage to get his name on the score sheet.

He would often get into positions where he looked all set to break his duck, but he'd either hit the woodwork or someone would make an extraordinary goal-line clearance. I think there was even a point where John Barnes' backside denied him a goal in a game at Leeds, so I think he was just destined not to score.

I tried to tee him up myself on countless occasions but it was just his *thing*. Everyone has something they don't achieve in life and Rob's was that elusive goal for Liverpool.

That said, I think it's important to remember that he was a defender first and foremost. It never, ever concerned any of us that he didn't score because he already offered so much to the team.

I can't remember a single mistake he made. He was always consistent and performed at a high level in spite of his injuries.

I was fortunate to play with some great players with England and Liverpool as well as the likes of the Brazilian Ronaldo, Raul and Zidane at Real Madrid. But the biggest tribute I can pay Rob is that I'll always regard him as one of the best teammates I ever had the privilege to line-up alongside.

He will always be someone I regard as a true gentleman and friend.

FOREWORD II:

ROBBIE FOWLER

"Macca, Carra, Souness, Ryan Giggs and you."

Those were the names that rolled off Trigger's tongue when he revealed the list of contributors for his book.

I had to laugh.

"What, no Noel Gallagher?" I asked.

He shook his head before offering that familiar, loveable chuckle.

It's a long-running joke, typical of the type of great banter we have had over the years.

I'm not sure how it all came about, but according to him he was once akin to an honorary member of Oasis.

He had been ruled out for several months with a back injury and claimed to have spent some time with them while they were on a mid-1990s tour of the UK.

None of us believed him, of course.

Even now he'll throw in the odd comment about his adventures with the Gallagher brothers. We still don't buy it!

He remains adamant though; he was big pals with Noel.

I recall repeatedly asking to see some proof of this unlikely friendship. He would always refer to a signed photograph they had given him that he had at home.

He kept telling us he would bring it to Melwood. It seemed rather convenient that it never made its much-anticipated appearance in West Derby.

It was all forgotten until one night myself and Macca jumped in the car and drove over the river to his house in Cheshire. We picked up Mark Wright on the way and were planning to have a low-key evening watching a match on TV.

We were sitting around in his living room having a cup of tea when I noticed the signed frame on the wall.

It was THE picture of Oasis with a message scrawled on the front. I looked a bit closer and burst out laughing.

It read: 'To Rob Jones from Noel Gallagher".

It was hardly the note you'd expect to get from a drinking buddy. Where was the personal touch?

As far as I could see, Noel had signed a very formal message, full titles and everything. It was the sort you'd expect him to give to a fan who turned up to a book signing - not his 'big chum'.

Naturally, we all ripped into Trig. He's never lived it down.

He insisted they were mates but I told him there was no way he was going to call him Rob Jones. He's Trig or Trigger to us, even nowadays, and you'd expect his big pal to call him Jonesy or something.

Anything but Rob Jones.

When I wrote my own book a few years ago, I mentioned that Trig was the man for the celebrities. It was nothing to do with the loathsome 'Spice boys' tag. It was all down to the Oasis autograph.

In a dressing room like Liverpool's you are going to get stick and, Trigger will tell you himself, he got more than most. But he's got a very dry sense of humour and his comebacks were always sharp. We knew he would never take anything to heart.

The Oasis tale simply illustrates what a good sport he is. It's also what makes him such a nice fella. We are still good mates now and speak regularly. A lot of people in the game have got so much time for him and I don't think you can pay any higher accolade than that. Just look at the list of names who have contributed to this book.

On the surface you would probably think he is very quiet. But when you get to know him, like I have over the years, he really comes out of his shell.

One of the first things you notice about him is his laugh. He's always giggling about something and is such an easy-going guy.

I was lucky enough to play with him at Liverpool and we were also in a number of England squads together. I'd say he was definitely up there as one of the best full-backs around. Not just in England. I'm talking world football.

I know Jason McAteer has something to say about that, but there's no doubt in my mind.

Not so long ago, we were all in the pub and the topic of best right-back came up. As usual, Trig and Dave (McAteer) rose to the bait.

We decided to get the definitive answer by texting 63336. You basically send an SMS question and they will reply with the answer. Usually it would be something like what is the capital of Outer Mongolia?

We asked who the better right-back was, Rob Jones or Jason McAteer?

It was hilarious. All these ex-Liverpool players were huddled around this one mobile phone waiting in anticipation for the response. It must have been a strange sight for the punters.

We gave it the big build up as you can imagine. Finally the answer arrived.

It was Trig.

You'd have thought McAteer had just missed a crucial penalty in the Champions League final. He was devastated.

Trig rarely gets over-excited but you could tell he was delighted.

For me, he was the complete full-back. He had bags of pace, he could defend and had a great engine to get forward.

As a striker it was fantastic to see him getting to the byline and putting quality crosses into the box. I'll never forget the day I got five goals at

Anfield in what was only my fourth senior game for Liverpool. It was a special moment in my career and, when I think back now, I can see that Trig played a big part in it.

He had a hand in a few of my goals. He must've watched it back on DVD recently because he made a point of reminding me!

It made me wonder just how many assists he chipped in with over his seven years with Liverpool. It must have been a fair amount.

Trig always supported the winger brilliantly and struck up a great understanding with Macca when he played on the right. I think he'd be a revelation nowadays because he had all of the attributes you want in a modern full-back.

The only thing he couldn't do was finish. If he was backing up the play or having to provide a killer pass, he was fine.

Shooting was another matter. In fact, if I'm honest, his finishing was terrible. If it wasn't for his missus I don't think he'd have ever scored! He must have spurned a raft of chances.

It may have never happened for him in the first-team but I'm delighted to say I was there the day he actually did net in a Liverpool shirt.

The landmark moment came when we were playing for the legends in the Masters tournament in Asia last summer. We've been competing in it for the past couple of years. It is a fantastic competition involving some great lads from the likes of Man United, Tottenham and a few other foreign teams.

I knew Trig was desperate to score. He'd always play it down, saying he wasn't bothered, but you could tell he wanted it.

It came against a Malaysian side and it wasn't the belter he'd have you believe either. But they all count, don't they?

I found myself presented with an open goal and glanced up to see Trig urging me to pass to him. As a striker your natural instinct is to score, so it took a lot of will power to lay it across and allow him to tap home.

It was worth it though. The joy on his face was a delight to behold.

I know a load of Kopites who stuck money on him as first goalscorer every week at 66/1. They used to ask if we had a special celebration ready if he did notch in the league.

You could tell they all wanted us to come up with something, but the answer was, no. That was simply because we knew he was never going to score. I told them it was just a waste of their hard-earned money!

We would have loved him to do it. Everyone on the pitch would have gone mental and the bookies would have taken a hiding. But it just wasn't meant to be.

When he retired at 27 he took a while to get back on his feet. He told me he had taken up shooting as a hobby to get him out and about.

I had to smile. He couldn't hit a barn door on the pitch and now he's telling me he's a sharp-shooter with a rifle. All I can picture is a clay pigeon soaring through the sky in slow motion before dropping to the floor with a thud, right next to a dozen he's already missed!

In all seriousness, he deserved a bit of luck when it all went wrong in football and I'm delighted he and his wife Sue set up a nursery business that is now flourishing. He's clearly a very clever and astute guy.

It's such a shame that his talent was cut short in his prime.

He would have got into any team in the league, if not any team in Europe at right back. That's how highly I rated Rob Jones.

He really was *that* good.

CHAPTER ONE

Butterflies and excitement.

The concoction of emotions gripped my stomach as I prepared for the biggest moment of my life.

The roar of over 40,000 supporters, the majority of which were baying for my blood, sent a tingling sensation throughout my body.

It was show time.

I glanced up to see Steve Nicol give me a quick nod and wink.

'What the hell was I doing here?'

The words kept circling my mind like vultures eager to pounce upon a prey that had wandered way out of its comfort zone.

Less than 48 hours earlier I had been a fourth division player with dreams and aspirations of one day making it in the big time.

Now I was here. Manchester United v Liverpool, one of the greatest matches in world football.

The jeers and cat whistles interrupted my train of thought as we ran out onto the magnificent playing surface. Old Trafford...

I was now a member of Liverpool's all-star squad. My boyhood heroes were teammates and I was about to go head-to-head with one of the hottest prospects in world football.

Ryan Giggs was already being hailed as the 'next George Best' and the snarling faces of the United supporters that flanked my touchline left me in no doubt that they were desperate to see him destroy me.

A sudden shift in the demeanour of those around me caught my attention.

It was time.

The referee put his whistle to his lips and the sharp shrill pierced my dreamlike state.

I took a deep intake of breath. This is what I had always dreamed of.

I glanced ahead and focused a steely gaze upon United's wing wizard. Determination and desire to succeed surged through my lungs as adrenalin kicked in.

The game kicked off and my nerves evaporated.

****

At the start of the 1991-92 campaign there was a decision to be made.

My contract with Crewe Alexandra was up in the summer and I had yet to be offered a new one.

I didn't think I was playing at the level I was capable of and at one point I was just going through the motions and getting through games.

It's a strange position to be in as a footballer and I don't know what would have transpired in the months ahead had it not been for a strange quirk of fate that would ultimately make my career.

I suppose I was very fortunate that the game Graeme Souness attended coincided with my return to form.

We had heard in the build up to a midweek League Cup encounter at home to Newcastle United that the Liverpool manager and his highly respected scout, Tom Saunders would be in the stands running the rule over one of our players.

It was already a big match but I know a few of the lads were even more eager to impress after news filtered through. The game itself turned out to be a classic but unfortunately for us, we were on the wrong end of a seven-goal thriller.

Despite conceding four goals I was happy with my overall performance. The fact that Souness had been in attendance hadn't really had any impact upon my game because I never imagined that they would have been looking at me.

I was playing left-back at the time but switched to right-back at the interval. I always preferred playing on my natural side. I could handle playing wide left but anyone will tell you that everything is far easier when you don't have to tackle with your wrong foot or cut inside to cross with it.

In the first period we won a free-kick on the left and I ran over and whipped it in with my right foot. We actually scored from it and Souness later told me that he had been really impressed by that. Of course if he had watched me in our previous games that season he'd have seen that I was very right-footed!

The next few days passed by without incident but as we arrived at the ground for a league game against Gillingham, it emerged that Liverpool's chief scout, Ron Yeats was there on Souness's behalf.

We went on to win 2-1 and again I didn't think anything of it until the following night.

I had just returned home from the shops and found a message on my answer machine from Crewe's manager, Dario Gradi asking me to give him a ring.

I was a bit shocked because he never rang any of us at home. I wasn't even sure he had my number! Obviously this was in the days when you didn't have mobile phones, so I quickly returned the call.

I can remember the conversation vividly. I was sitting on the staircase when he told me Liverpool had been in touch.

- They want you to head up there tomorrow and sign for them.

I was stunned and struggled to find the words to respond.

Dario must have taken this to mean I was concerned about leaving Crewe.

- Don't worry. If you don't want to go or they don't give you the money you want then we will take you back.

I'm sure my response was polite at the time but inside I was just thinking 'yeah, right!'

The team I had supported all of my life, England's most successful football club was interested in me. There was no way I would quibble over money!

We had a guy at the club called Kenny Swain who actually went on to become the oldest player to play for Crewe. He'd also won the European Cup with Aston Villa in his prime and he had taught me an awful lot during my first few years with the Alex.

Dario told me that Kenny knew Souness quite well and that he would pick me up on the Friday morning and take me over to Anfield.

My mind was in a complete whirl. With all due respect to Dario I just wanted to get off the phone and scream. When I did finally hang up I burst out crying. I was that emotional. It was a huge shock more than anything.

I'd never have dreamt that Liverpool would come calling, especially when you think of all the clubs and players out there.

But it was true.

Liverpool. *My* team, wanted to sign me.

In a way I was lucky because I had upped my level and played very well in the two games they had attended.

It's all very well saying that you are a talented footballer and you are always going to make it, but I think you need that little bit of fortune too.

If Souness had come to watch me a month or so earlier I may not have been playing at my peak and not made enough of an impression.

That's something that struck me more in hindsight. At the time I was just overjoyed that I was heading to Merseyside.

Even when I had been playing for Crewe I would still go on the Kop and watch Liverpool. If we didn't have a game on a Wednesday night, and the Reds did, then I would jump on the train with my mates and watch my heroes in action.

To suddenly go from worshipping all those international stars to playing five-a-side with them at Melwood was just unbelievable. But that was what lay ahead, so long as I didn't mess up when I went to meet Graeme and Tom.

Kenny Swain had been great with me at Crewe and something he said to me en route to Liverpool has always stuck in my mind. He told me that whatever Liverpool offered, I should just nod my head and grab the pen!

He chuckled as he said it but I've no doubt he was deadly serious.

There were four of us in the room that would ultimately be the place where all my childhood dreams would come true. Kenny, Souness, Tom and myself.

We chatted about football for a while and Souness asked me what salary I was on at Crewe. I told him it was £250 per week. He said that Liverpool would double that and asked what I thought of it. I just said yes straight away. I didn't have an agent but I was more than happy with that. At that point I'd have played for free! I was 19 and just wanted to be able to call myself a Liverpool player.

When it was all agreed Souness turned to me and told me to get changed for training. In those days the players used to get a bus from Anfield to Melwood, the club's training ground.

The lads had already gone so I was handed some kit and told that we would sign the contract after the session.

Souness drove me over there. Unsurprisingly I was a bit nervous as we pulled through the gates.
Ronnie Moran was already putting the rest of the players through some exercises as we pulled up.

Souness gathered everyone around and introduced me. I could feel the eyes of Ray Houghton, Ian Rush, Steve McMahon and Steve Nicol all centred upon yours truly.

It was a huge moment for me and they were all very nice. I'm sure they'd seen loads of up-and-coming kids sign over the years so they probably weren't that interested. I was a nobody and they were just keen to get one of their famous five-a-side matches underway.

So this was it. Time to impress. The nerves went out the window because I knew that I couldn't be found wanting. I needed to take my chance. I told myself that Souness must have thought something of me to bring me in and put me straight into training with these legends.

One of the first touches I had was one I would never forget. McMahon came flying in on me from nowhere and lunged forward with the type of two-footed challenge that would earn an instant red card nowadays.

I managed to ride it and got on with the game. Once I came to know McMahon I realised this was just typical of his appetite for football. He wanted to test me out and see if I had anything about me.

It didn't faze me and at the end of the session I thought I had done well. The players all jumped back on the coach to Anfield while I travelled back in Souness's car.

It was during that short drive that he mentioned the small matter of Liverpool's next match. A trip to Old Trafford on Sunday.

- We've got Manchester United this weekend. It's a big game... How do you think you would cope?

I was startled but quickly regained my composure. There was no way I was going to come across like I wasn't ready.

- I think I'd be fine with it. I wouldn't have a problem.

- Great, because I'm thinking of putting you in the team to mark Ryan Giggs.

It transpired that Souness had heard about a competition that ran throughout the Football League where they were trying to find the fastest player in England. I had been put forward from Crewe and had done well in it.

He continued.

- How would you cope against Giggs and his pace?

Again I tried to remain as calm as possible.

- I'll be fine. I'm ready for it.

I managed to keep the tone of my voice level but inside the butterflies were whipping up a storm.

It was at this moment that we arrived back at Anfield. He paused and looked me straight in the eye. I smiled back and held his gaze.

He didn't say anything. He just nodded, opened the car door and told me to join the other lads in the canteen.

My heart was pounding. I just hoped my expression had told him whatever it was he wanted to see.

I met up with the others for lunch and then Ronnie Moran came and spoke to me about what I needed to do in preparation for the match.

I was supposed to be playing for Crewe on the Saturday on a pitch that had probably seen better days. That was all about to change. I was going to be staying overnight in Manchester ahead of one of the biggest matches in world football.

Liverpool had endured a few injuries in the early stages of the season and it was the absence of Barry Venison that led to me having a shot at a starting berth.

Fortunately, I didn't have too much time to worry about it. I rushed home and got all my bags packed. On the Saturday morning I arrived at Melwood for a light training session before joining the rest of the team on the coach to Manchester. I got a few quizzical looks and smirks. I'd brought my own towel and training kit as that was the norm at Crewe. I soon realised that it wasn't the case at Liverpool.

It was a bit surreal. Ronnie Moran was pottering about asking us what we wanted for our pre-match meals and I just couldn't get my head around the fact that this was now going to be my life.

We stayed at the Cottons Hotel & Spa in Knutsford that night. The players were great with me and everything seemed to be moving along nicely until we had our evening meal.

I was sat in silence while the usual banter was flying around the tables. I had Dean Saunders opposite and McMahon to my side.

McMahon was a nice enough bloke but he wasn't the type that you'd mess with. Nor was he the kind of guy that would look to make you feel welcome as a newcomer. I would also come to realise that Deano was a bit of a joker too.

Liverpool's record signing at the time asked me to pour him some water. Naturally, I was eager to fit in so I was happy to oblige. He was holding his glass over McMahon's plate and as I began to pour it, he jerked his arm away. I could only look on in horror as the water splashed all over McMahon's meal.

There was a brief moment of silence before everyone started laughing - with the exception of McMahon. I tried to apologise but the words just came out as gibberish. I was just trying to keep my head down and get through my first few days unscathed but all of a sudden I was in the spotlight.

Looking back on it I think it was a good thing. It released some tension and everyone had a little joke with me about it. Luckily enough they had enough food to provide McMahon with a new meal too.

Having survived the steely gaze of one of Liverpool's hardest ever players, I opted to get an early night in alongside my roommate for the trip, Mark Walters.

Wally was a quiet guy so that suited me perfectly after what had just happened. I rang home to speak to my Mum and my step-dad, Paul. I had received two tickets from the club and they were going to be at the game the following day.

Paul told me that he'd been in a bit of a daze since he got the news and had made a huge mistake when he had gone to a petrol station in Rossmore. He'd filled up his tank but in his haste to get home had just driven off without realising! It was only when he got back and there was a knock on the door that it dawned on him. When he told the copper why he wasn't quite with it, he was understanding and told him to just go and pay!

My biological dad, Pete flew over from Jersey too. He managed to get some tickets off a tout so that he and his mates could watch it. He was determined to be there even if it was from the United end!

He'd actually had trials at Liverpool when he was younger but hadn't made the cut. He later went on to play for a team in Jersey, so I suppose we have some decent 'football genes' in our family.

As I lay in the darkness of the hotel room, my mind continued to race with scenarios. To be fair to Souness he was taking an almighty gamble by picking me. He had only really seen me play a couple of times.

It's a bit of a blur looking back at the day of the match.

I got on the team bus and recall turning up at Old Trafford with my stomach in knots. Things were being thrown at us as we pulled into the ground. Fans were flicking v-signs and calling us every name under the sun.
If you ever wanted an example for using the phrase 'baptism of fire', then this was it! I remember briefly wishing to make my debut in an easier game.

That soon faded as we stepped out on to the pitch for the warm-up. Ask any player what games they want to play in and they will tell you it is the big encounters they relish the most. I may have still been a teenager but there was no doubt I was up for this.

As we gathered in the changing room it dawned upon me that the other players didn't know the team yet. Souness had only told me given the circumstances. He had recognised that I needed time to prepare myself mentally. It was the biggest day of my life.

I don't know if anyone was surprised to hear my name read out. I wasn't looking around at that point. My eyes were fixed on the floor. To be blunt, I was tucked away in the corner shitting myself.

Once again Deano was sat next to me. I don't know if he was doing it on purpose to try and take my mind off it but he kept taking the piss out of the way I was dressed. I was taking my trousers off and had these football shorts on underneath. He hammered me for wearing them.

There were roars of laughter until Deano gave me the lifeline I needed when he suggested that they could be my lucky shorts.

I seized upon the explanation and with footballers being footballers, the superstition was greeted by nods of approval. They may not have been lucky shorts beforehand but if I got through the afternoon unscathed they soon would be.

That incident took up the majority of the pre-match talk and before I knew it, I'd pulled on the number five shirt and I was walking out in front of a packed Old Trafford crowd. I was acutely aware that the majority wanted nothing more than to see me endure 90 minutes of severe torment against their hero, Giggs.

I knew the match was on TV but as I ran through my last minute warm-ups it was the last thing on my mind. All I was thinking about was defending.

If I did my job and stuck with my man then I would be halfway there.

And that's all I did.

I think I got a nice touch of the ball early on and then I won a header against Giggs.

It gave me great confidence and that's when the adrenalin and your natural ability as a footballer kicks in.

A good example came midway through the first half when Giggs rushed to put me under pressure in my own penalty area. I tried a Cruyff turn and managed to get beyond him and clear the ball up field.

He tried to knock it past me and outpace me a few times but I was quick and always managed to recover. I don't know what it was but I just seemed to suit playing against him.

I think Alex Ferguson must have told Giggs to get at me as much as possible and test me out but as the half time whistle went it was still goalless. As far as I was concerned I'd not been made a mug of.

In the dressing room Souness spoke to the team and after that he tapped me on the back and just said, 'same again.'

Roy Evans told me to keep doing what I was already doing and that was all they could ask for. They didn't want to complicate things, which was fine by me.

We started the second half quite well but I could feel myself getting tired. My body was starting to cramp up and when the late Gary Ablett was sent off just after the hour mark, Souness must have decided he needed fresh legs.

I was replaced by Mike Marsh after a 65-minute debut for Liverpool. It wasn't just the running that I had done in the match. The days leading up to the game, knowing that I was going to play, had created a tension in my muscles. It was the right call for me to go off.

I would often get cramp in the years that would follow especially during big games because of the pressure of being involved in such high profile matches.

The rest of the lads saw the game out for a creditable 0-0 draw and the hosts couldn't contain their frustration. Mark Hughes's late red card a case in point.

As we made a satisfied walk back towards the changing room the coaching staff seemed happy with me.

It was a creditable draw but this was Liverpool Football Club and no-one was getting carried away with a point, even if we had managed it with a patched up side.

I later found out that Gordon Strachan was in the studio for ITV that day and he had revealed that Ferguson had sent him to watch me as a scout. He said that he had told the United boss that I was a decent enough player but said that I had no pace! He then added that once Ferguson had seen how quick I was it was pretty much the end of his scouting days at United!

It was a tongue in cheek way of saying that he had made a mistake. Not that I'd have joined United anyway. I was a red.

When I got home that night my muscles were killing me and it wasn't long before I was asleep. Moving from the old fourth division up to the first division is one thing, but going straight in at the deep end against Manchester United and Giggs is probably about 10 levels up!

Now the big challenge was to do it week in, week out.

It was one I couldn't wait to meet head on.

CHAPTER TWO

- "Crossed in again towards Dalglish... he's done it again!"

The words roared from my lips as I reeled away in celebration of yet another wonder goal scored in the salubrious surroundings of Summertrees Road.

Of course, Liverpool's iconic number seven may not have set foot in Ellesmere Port but when I was growing up he happened to be something of a regular in our back yard.

My sister, Kate lay face down in the mud. She was four years younger than me and hardly enthused by her role as a makeshift goalkeeper. She was a poor-man's Bruce Grobbelaar, but hey, I had to work with what I had.

In later years she would be dragged along to my junior level matches at Crewe and she still jokes now that she played a role in my rise to prominence as a footballer. I always retort that she couldn't have been that good because I never scored for Liverpool!

Back in 1979 she was my adversary as the lush green grass at number two bore witness to regular reconstructions of King Kenny's latest piece of magic. In my mind's eye it was our very own private Anfield.

They didn't have names and numbers on the back of shirts then, but if they had, my mud-splattered kit would almost certainly have sported the name 'Dalglish'.

Kenny had become my big hero.

The King's picture graced every spec of my wall space and I was lucky enough to get a signed photo of him thanks to my granddad, Bill.

Even when you see Kenny now he has this aura about him. He was an incredible player.

I remember meeting him for the first time. It was a few years after I'd joined Liverpool. I think he had come to Melwood to watch some training. I'm not sure he even knew who I was but it was a major thrill for me to speak to the man who had been my idol all those years ago in Summertrees Road.

Kenny was my hero but perhaps unsurprisingly, it was my granddad Bill, a former Reds player in his own right, who introduced me to the wonders of Liverpool Football Club.

He took me to my first game when I was eight. From that moment on I was hooked.

It was a Boxing Day encounter against Manchester United at Anfield and the players served up the perfect, belated Christmas present. Alan Hansen and David Johnson were on the score sheet in a 2-0 win.

I suppose it was fate that my first match as both a player and a fan would be against one of the club's biggest rivals.

Having once graced the Anfield pitch as a player, there was only one part of the ground my granddad was ever going to take me. The match may have passed me by but the intense pride I felt at being one with the famous Kop was something I'll never forget.

At that moment I knew what I wanted from life.

Not only did I want to follow in granddad's footsteps and play for Liverpool, I wanted to be Kenny Dalglish!

Okay, the latter part may have been somewhat impossible but I knew then that my destiny was to become a professional footballer. Maybe it was written in the stars too. When I was born granddad Bill and grandma Vera brought some miniature football boots that had been hanging around their car's rear view mirror to the hospital.

They put it on my cot as a gift, leading the nurses to say, 'Oh, how cute. I guess this one's going to be a footballer!'

Little did they know how right they were!

Apparently there was a fair bit of banter flying around between the two sets of grandparents back then.

My mum's dad, granddad Joe, had grown up on Scotland Road and he was an avid Evertonian along with my nana Peggy. They hoped I would grow up to play for the Blues, but obviously my dad's side of the family were all Reds.

Despite the rivalry they were all great friends and when I signed for Liverpool, Joe was made up for me, regardless of his passion for the Toffees.

Sadly my grandma Vera and nana Peggy both died when I was young, so they never got to see me play for Liverpool. They would have been so proud.

I suppose it was only natural that Bill's past exploits with the Reds would put him in the driving seat when it came to deciding on the venue for my first experience of a match and a Boxing Day fixture at Anfield became the ritual for us.

My biological dad, Pete would come along too and that made it extra special as I didn't see him as often as I wanted to. He and my mum, Joan, had split up when I was just a baby. Pete had wanted a fresh start so he moved to Jersey with some friends. I only saw him during the summer and at Christmas but he was always there for me if I needed him.

Mum then met my step-dad, Paul and within a few years they had married. As far as I'm concerned I've got two great dads and I get the best of both worlds. To this day I refer to Paul as 'dad' because he was there for me 24/7. I had a real issue with calling them by their Christian names in this book because I've always thought of them both as 'Dad'.

However, after speaking with them about it, I thought it would be best to call them that, to avoid confusion over whom I was referring to. They were fine with it and again it shows what great guys they are.

So Paul was there for me day-to-day and I would get the treat of a holiday to Jersey with my granddad Bill and grandma Vera every summer to see Pete.

I always loved my granddad's company. Quite often we would say very little, but there was just something about his presence that felt magical.

When I made the decision to write this book a few years ago, one of the first things I wanted to do was to speak to him about his career with the Reds. Sadly he passed away on Boxing Day, 2010 so we didn't have the opportunity to have an in-depth talk.

He had always been such a quiet man, a true gentleman who rarely spoke about his achievements. When I would ask him about his time in L4 he would never go into any great detail.

- "What was it like playing with the great Billy Liddell?

- "He was a real joker in the dressing room. A great man and an incredible player.

But that was it. Granddad was a man of few words; very modest and humble.

I acquired much of my knowledge about his Reds career from his old scrapbooks. There wasn't much, but then that was him all over.

Even when I marvelled at his medal of bravery from World War II he would always play his heroics down.

He had been involved in a particularly intense battle that had seen a couple of his comrades wounded behind enemy lines. The orders had been to fall back, but my granddad refused to give up.

He crawled his way back into the danger zone, evading bullet after bullet to pull off a miraculous solo rescue mission.

He had risked his life without a moment's hesitation and was quite rightly awarded a medal. Not that you would know that from talking to him. His response to any praise was that anyone would have done the same thing.

My son Declan has the medal now and it is one of his most cherished possessions.

Granddad Bill may have been a somewhat taciturn character but I loved the time I spent with him as a youngster.

He used to take me with him to watch games he was scouting. It's well documented that he 'found' Roger Hunt and 'Sir Roger' went on to win a World Cup with England, so he didn't have a bad track record did he? I still see Roger occasionally too. We meet up with some of the lads for the Liverpool former players Christmas meal and he always speaks fondly of the man who spotted him in action for Stockton Heath.

Granddad also did a few reports on Ian Rush. I could sit here and make out I was with him the day he identified 'Tosh' as a future Reds legend, but to be honest I have no idea whether I was there or not.

It would be a wonderful story wouldn't it? The little kid kicking a ball on the sidelines the day my granddad watched Rushie would one day go on to play in the same side as our all-time record goalscorer.

But I was far too young to recall it, and if I'm honest, I don't think it happened.

People ask me if my granddad played a big part in my career because they assumed he must have imparted some pearls of wisdom. Again, it would make for a good story if he had pulled me to one side after a match and analysed my game. But it wasn't the case.

That's not to say he didn't take a keen interest. When I first started playing as a kid he was always on the sidelines, quietly cheering me on. Rain, wind or snow he would turn out to see me in action. It was the same with my parents. I can't remember a game when they weren't there to support me. That continued right through my career too.

When I read about granddad's career now I wish I had learned more from him in person.

He signed for Liverpool in 1938 but the start of World War II meant that his debut was delayed until the opening day of the 1946-47 season, when he played in a 1-0 win at Sheffield United.

He was a very versatile player who was just as comfortable in central defence as he was in midfield. I've heard some fans of an older generation suggest he was the Jamie Carragher of his day and I think that is a nice comparison.

I wish there was more television footage from that era so I could sit back and watch him in action but unfortunately I've yet to find any.

Like I say, he didn't talk about his Liverpool career at all. Even when my son, Declan asked him he would always give one-word answers.

He played 32 times in all competitions for that famous title-winning team of 1947 and scored two in a 7-4 win over Chelsea at Anfield. It remains one of the greatest matches of the time but it was perhaps his appearance in the 1950 FA Cup final that stands out.

The sight of his name on the team sheet apparently caused quite a stir on the day of the Wembley showdown as he was involved and Bob Paisley wasn't. That's the only thing I can remember him talking about when I was a kid.

As I was growing up Bob was the manager and I remember sitting next to granddad at the match as he sang the praises of the man wearing a flat cap in the dugout. He told me he was delighted to see Paisley doing so well as he had played with him in the same Liverpool team. They were big pals.

He said Paisley had scored in the 2-0 semi-final win over Everton and was expected to play in the final against Arsenal. My granddad was also involved against the Toffees but it was suggested that Kay had picked my granddad over Paisley at Wembley.

Liverpool went on to lose 2-0 although my granddad almost salvaged something for the Reds when he headed against the crossbar with the score finely poised at 1-0 to the Gunners.

My grandma Vera was actually pregnant when she attended the game. Pete was born not long after and she often joked that she could have had her son at Wembley. I'm sure my Dad would have loved that!

I've still got the shirt granddad wore in that final. I've also got the programme and I keep them in a safe place at home. In our old house we used to have a sports bar and they took pride of place in a glass case there. Now he's gone, I'll cherish them even more.

He also played twice for England in victories over Portugal and Belgium in the lead up to the 1950 World Cup finals. I think one of his big regrets was that he didn't get the nod for that tournament.

His time at Liverpool never reached the heights of that FA Cup final appearance again and it was a shame that his final season with the Reds ended in relegation in the 1953-54 campaign.

I think we are the only grandson and granddad to have played for Liverpool and that's a nice statistic for the family.

On the odd occasion that I won a monthly award the club brought granddad on to the pitch with me to make the presentation. It was a great touch and a really proud moment. I can remember one in particular just prior to a match with Southampton when I had won the Young Eagle of the month award.

A photo was taken and I've still got it now, buried away with a whole lot of other memorabilia. I was actually quite surprised that the club convinced him to go along and stand in the spotlight.

Out of all of us he had taken the fact I had signed for Liverpool well and truly in his stride. He had refused to come to watch at first, joking that it was bad for his heart and that he'd be better off doing the gardening!

But deep down, I knew he was delighted.

Attending matches with my granddad when I was a scrawny kid was a real thrill.

It quickly whet my appetite and I began to take a real interest in the playing side of the game. The path to L4 started with a local Ellesmere Port side by the name of Polygon. I was a box-to-box midfielder in my younger days and, believe it or not, used to love getting forward and scoring goals! We won a lot of trophies and were probably one of the best teams in Cheshire.

They have since changed their name to Ellesmere Port Youth, partly because they play at the town's well-known youth centre. There were actually suggestions they might build a supermarket there a few years back and I had the local newspaper, the Pioneer, phoning me up asking me to give them a quote opposing the move.

Fortunately nothing came of it but if anything I said helped in some way then I'm glad. It's the place where it all started for me so I was only too happy to lend a hand.

My weekends may have been occupied by my adventures with Polygon but Monday to Friday was spent at Meadow Junior School.

My favourite subject was PE. There was a teacher by the name of Mr Holden and he was as dedicated as they come. He was a really nice man. He saw I had great potential as a sportsman straight away.

He got me involved in anything he could and as a result I was representing the school in pretty much everything we entered, from athletics to football.

I was particularly good at cricket. I was a fast bowler who was quite handy with a bat and for a while it was a case of choosing between that and football. I even held the school record at one point. I think it was 76 runs in 20 overs. I don't know if it still stands but I remember being at the crease smashing sixes for fun.

We'd play matches where the teachers took on the pupils and I'd always have them running for cover. They feared me because I was a mean bowler!

It probably won't surprise you to learn that I was a quiet lad growing up. If you are looking for some anecdotes about my bad boy days in the Port then you are reading the wrong book.

I remember my Mum going up for parents evening and telling me what one of my teachers, Mr Furber, had said when she asked him if I was behaving well at school. Apparently he just looked at her in shock and said that he actually wished that one day I would be a bit naughty!

It was an odd thing to say but I think he just wanted to get some reaction from me. I rarely contributed in class discussion and he probably wondered if he was failing to help me realise my potential.

I was a bit of a goody-two-shoes but, to be fair, I don't see the problem with that. I had respect for my teachers and my classmates and was always pretty popular at school.

I had developed childhood migraine from the age of three and I also had asthma so maybe that explained why I was so quiet. I had a lot to deal with and we made a point of keeping my problems with migraines to ourselves.

It was quite rare to have it as bad as I had it as a toddler and I had to undergo countless tests which was a really worrying time for my parents. There was even talk that I may have had a brain tumour so it was quite serious.

I would be playing in the garden and all of a sudden I would race into the house screaming. It would last up to seven days at a time and leave me vomiting, with an adversity to light.

I would be lying in a dark room for a week or two and as a result I would end up losing a lot of weight. It was a tough time in my life and it only began to improve when I turned 11.

In those days the medication wasn't what it is today and it rarely did much for me.

I slowly learned to cope with it and would sometimes play matches suffering with the pain. I could often be seen running up and down the pitch holding my eye because the light was affecting me.

That was bad enough but the asthma made life extra difficult.

I never really shook that off. Even when I was playing regularly for Liverpool, I would be coughing and spitting up fluid throughout a game. That was the type of asthma I had. It wasn't really full blown or at the point where you couldn't catch your breath. In fact, it wasn't until I went to Crewe that the medics noticed I had the problem and diagnosed it as asthma.

I'd take an inhaler before matches and that would generally do the trick.

As for the migraines, they eventually stopped at the age of 14 but if they had continued then I don't think I would have gone on to play for Liverpool.

I missed a lot of school as a result of it and sometimes I'd be missing for as many as two weeks out of every four. Inevitably my studies suffered and my grades were never particularly great.

Not that I was overly concerned with my academic career. It was sport all the way for me.

We had a cracking football team and won a lot of the local tournaments.

In fact, the side was so well respected that when I moved up to Whitby Comprehensive they eventually decided to break with tradition and start up a team. It had been a big rugby school up to that point but because we had won so many trophies as juniors, they eventually gave in to the clamour and entered us into competition. All of the parents of the kids who enjoyed such great success at Meadow signed a petition and eventually the school caved.

That was in my third year there - Year 9 nowadays.

I remember I was picked for one of the England youth sides and my mum had to go up to see the head teacher to convince them that I should be given the opportunity to go and play. I was at an age where you still needed permission from the school and they were always somewhat awkward.

The head teacher argued that if I was willing to put as much effort into my rugby as with my football then I would have a chance of reaching the highest level in that sport instead. That's the type of stubborn attitude I was up against at first.

Eventually they would relent and I continued to succeed in a number of sports. I had options in terms of what career I wanted to pursue but then Crewe Alexandra came knocking.

In my last two years at Whitby High there had been a teacher's strike on after-school activity. That meant no sport and most importantly, no football.

It could have denied me the opportunity to show the world what I could do but a teacher from Helsby High School by the name of Dennis Evans stepped in.

Dennis had known my Dad, Pete, from his playing days in the Port. He received a phone call from one of his scouting friends who convinced him I was worth having a look at. So he asked me to come along and play in a match for a team he ran by the name of Halton Boys.

It just so happened that the game he invited me to play in was against one of Crewe's youth sides. We actually lost the match 9-2 but I felt I had produced a good individual display.

Crewe's first-team manager, Dario Gradi had watched the action from the sidelines along with youth team coach Barry Burnell.

They decided they wanted to have another look at me and spoke to my parents just after the full-time whistle. The conversation was a very positive one and not long after that they asked me to join the Crewe Academy.

When I later signed for Liverpool I actually went back to Halton Boys along with Dario to present them with £400 worth of tracksuits. It was Dario's way of thanking Dennis for his role in helping to spot me, which was a great touch.

It was nothing new for Dario to be there on the day I played for Halton. In recent years I have taken my son Declan to the Crewe Academy and he's still there on the sidelines casting his eye over the Railwaymen of the future.

It just shows the dedication of the man. He lives and breathes football.

Most parents would have jumped at the chance to sign their child up with a professional football club, but mine were always very careful and supportive. They had already turned down approaches from the likes of Southampton and Wolves after the respective clubs had seen me in action for Cheshire Schools.

They also had the advantage of being able to call upon the expertise of my granddad Bill. I know they spoke to him at length about whether Crewe was the right club for me. There are always rumours that bigger sides could be monitoring you, but granddad was aware of the reputation Crewe were developing at youth level and felt they could be the best fit for me. After some deliberation, we all decided it would be the best place for me to progress.

My parents' commitment to supporting my career must have cost them a fortune in petrol over the years. Paul used to have a book of all of the football league grounds and he would tick off the ones he and my mum went to. They had been to 76 out of 92 by the time I had finished playing.

I remember one time Mum and Paul travelled down to watch Crewe play an FA Cup tie at Chelsea and they bumped into Dario. He didn't say much to them but when the Crewe Chronicle newspaper came out the following week he had written a massive column about how they were an example to all parents involved in youth football.

It was a fantastic piece and I know they were very proud of it.

Their decision to give Crewe the green light paid off straight away and a week after impressing on trial I signed schoolboy terms. I settled into the set-up pretty quickly.

It wasn't long before I was earning good reports for the U15s and any thoughts of being the next Ian Botham were slowly fading away.

My life was all about school and football, with a heavy emphasis on the latter!

I remember the careers officer sitting me down when I was 14 and asking me what I hoped to do with my life. I told him I was going to be a professional footballer. He didn't take my reply very seriously and asked if I had a back up in mind. I insisted there was no need. I knew what I wanted to do.

That may have come across as cocky and naïve but having missed so much school, football was all I knew. I was committed to making my dream a reality.

I was making good progress too and during the 1987-88 campaign I took another major step forward when I was called into the squad for the FA Youth Cup.

I was now playing two years above my age group and relishing the challenge. I was the sweeper in a team that included winger Neil Harris, striker Steve Walters, Rob Edwards, Neil Morton and Colin Rose.

My pace made me the perfect player to mop up anything played in-behind the full-backs and I had no trouble settling into the role.

Barry Burnell and Paul McCann shared the coaching duties with the youth team and it was a fantastic set up.

Paul was part-time but he was really approachable. John Fleece helped out too and later went on be the club's kit man. Sadly, he passed away last year and I attended his funeral with my step-Dad, Paul. He was a great guy and really helped me when I first joined Crewe as a young lad. We'd often go through John if we wanted to ask Dario something but were too scared to face him!

We went on to have some great nights in the Youth Cup that season. We would run out at Gresty Road and there would be four or five thousand fans there to cheer us on. Not bad for a bunch of teenagers!

I savoured every moment of those nights.

We played 12 games in total and beat the likes of Tranmere, Aston Villa and Middlesbrough en route to the semi-finals.

We had a good, solid team and we started to believe we could go all of the way until we came up against eventual winners, Arsenal.

I remember I had to mark the Gunners' future first-team striker Kevin Campbell in both legs of the tie. He was a big lad even then and don't forget he was a couple of years older than me too!

We gave a good account of ourselves in a 1-1 draw at Gresty Road but were completely overwhelmed at Highbury.

We lost 6-2 on aggregate but it was still a great experience for us.

Our run to the last four hadn't gone unnoticed either. There were an increasing number of scouts at our matches and I think it was around this time that people were starting to realise something special was happening in Crewe's youth system.

It's well documented that the likes of David Platt came through under Dario's watchful eye. Unfortunately I never got to play with him at Crewe because he left just before I came onto the first-team scene.

When you think of some of the talent that has emerged, the names really do just roll off the tongue.

Craig Hignett, Geoff Thomas, Danny Murphy, Neil Lennon and Robbie Savage – all these players owe a lot of their success to their Crewe Alexandra origins.

Even now, I'm well aware that my rapid rise to the top all came about as a result of the way Dario and his staff helped to nurture me.

I know he had various offers to move on to bigger clubs but he remained loyal and happy with his role at Crewe. He did things the way he wanted to and there was no guarantee that it would be the case if he moved onto pastures new.

All of the big clubs have Academies nowadays but Crewe was light years ahead of the rest back then.

Despite our success that year, the majority of that team ended up being released. We were a good unit but there weren't many individuals in there.

I was still two years younger than most of those guys and was seen as one of the more promising players. When I look back now I'm so happy I made the choice to go to Crewe. I was given the chance to gain experience at such a young age and that was invaluable.

Playing in the Youth Cup in front of large crowds and on a big stage like Highbury had made me determined to keep progressing as fast as I could.

The Railwaymen didn't really have much in terms of a reserve team so the next step in my development was the big one.

A first-team debut.

CHAPTER THREE

- 'You want me to play right-back?'

The question slipped off my tongue with an incredulity I instantly regretted.

It was my secondary reaction to the news that I was being picked for my first appearance in senior football.

The initial one was obviously one of great elation as the culmination of all of those years of hard work moved to within touching distance.

The only problem was that I had *never* played full-back before.

My rise to prominence at Crewe had seen me evolve from the box-to-box midfielder that had excelled with Polygon, into a solid defender with good vision and pace to burn.

I had assumed that would be where I would make my bow.

I was wrong.

- 'You've got everything you need to play at right-back. That's your long-term future. You'll do great. Trust me.

Dario's reassurance helped quell my initial concern. As usual, he was proved right.

I made my first-team debut on Saturday, April 9, 1988 in a 3-1 win at home to Darlington.

It was the realisation of the club's long-term plan for me. At first I was a bit puzzled, but Dario told me that I would eventually be one of the country's best right-backs and that they had been playing me in the centre to prepare me for what lay ahead.

I had slotted into defence with relative ease and when I did come undone my pace usually got me out of trouble.

Dario had explained that he saw my involvement as part of a learning curve and that he didn't see me fighting for a first-team spot just yet. Despite that, I received some positive praise from the press following my debut, not only for my performance but because I became the youngest player to feature for Crewe in 30 years.

In fact, I became the second youngest in the club's history at the age of 16 years and 158 days. A forward by the name of David Jones held the record after he made his bow back in 1956.

I was delighted to make such rapid progress and although I was substituted on 75 minutes, I was buzzing that night. I'd made a decent contribution overall and even managed to hook a goal-bound effort from Darlington's Kevin Stonehouse off the line.

I'd gone off with cramp and woke up a bit sore the next day. That soon faded into insignificance when I saw the local paper. Dario had singled me out for special praise and suggested that the team had not been as strong after I had left the field of play.

That was music to my ears. For some lads it may have gone to their heads but that was never an issue with me.

It wasn't my style to act all flash. I was still living at home with my parents and that kept my feet on the ground. I had understood from an early age that I couldn't be going out getting drunk with my mates on a Friday night. There was usually a game to play on the Saturday, so I was always tucked up in bed nice and early.

I think the only thing anyone could level at me was that I never cleaned my boots! Paul had cleaned and polished them from when I first started out and it became a bit of a ritual that he did them.

I know that sounds bad but I think that secretly he quite liked doing it too!

I remember Colin Rose turned up with filthy boots for an U15 game once and the coach wouldn't let him play. When I went home I told Paul and we both had a chuckle about it. If it wasn't for him, maybe I would have missed some important games where I went on to impress!

There were only a few games left that season and I was handed some opportunities. Dario had made his intentions clear, that he wanted to give some of the lads from the Youth Cup team a chance.

We drew our next two matches against Cambridge and Stockport before a game at Tranmere Rovers that caused a bit of an issue at school.

The match was scheduled to kick off at 7.30pm and my Mum and Dad let me take the day off so I could relax before it. They rang the school and told them I had the flu.

In hindsight that was a silly move as anyone could have seen me playing. It didn't even occur to me that evening and I put in another decent performance in a hard-fought 2-2 draw.

I was still reliving bits of the game in my head when I walked through the school gates the following day, only to be brought right back down to earth when I received a message telling me I had to go and see the headmaster.

It still didn't click, but going to see the head is never good news, is it?

I walked in and he was very friendly at first.

- How's your flu?

-Fine thanks, much better now.

I felt relieved. Maybe he was just checking to make sure I was well enough to return to school.

-Funny that. I was at the Tranmere versus Crewe game last night. There was someone who looked just like you running up and down the wing!

I felt my cheeks grow hot and inflamed. I was about to hit him with a flood of excuses when he broke the tension with a warm smile.

-Look. It's okay. But you can't do that in the future. You need to talk to me. I could have stopped you playing. School must come first.

He let me off the hook but not before I had written him a grovelling apology promising I would never do it again.

Looking back it was a bit naïve. What if I had chalked up a hat-trick?

I'd have been all over the papers for my goal-scoring heroics. Maybe that's why I only ever scored two goals in my career, to avoid getting caught out!

The head teacher was right about my education of course. School should always come first, but at the age of 16 I was just looking to serve my time and focus on Crewe.

I didn't feature in the final three matches of the season as Dario decided it was time to put me back in the youth team. It was slightly frustrating to be honest but I knew he had my best interests at heart.

He'd been playing me in three different positions and told me not to take my demotion as a sign I hadn't done well for him. He told me I looked like I already belonged in the fourth division and that he was delighted with what I had done for his side.

I had gained so much confidence from my brief flirtation with the first-team and when I left school in the summer I signed my YTS forms straight away.

Dario called my parents and asked if he could come to the house to discuss the contract.

We gathered in the living room to wait for him, but he was already running late which was very unlike him.

Next minute, the phone rang. It was Dario. He was lost down what he described as a never-ending lane in Stoke! He'd gone completely the wrong way.

When he did eventually arrive he had this huge mobile phone with him. We were all really impressed because no-one had them back in those days. That still sticks in my mind now.

We were also wondering why he had chosen to come in person. A lot of the lads were being offered YTS forms and none of them were getting this type of treatment.

The long and short of it was that on top of the YTS forms he wanted to make sure that they signed me on professional terms as soon as I was old enough. He wasn't a contract type of guy. He operated on the premise that if you shook hands on a deal that was it. It was binding.

He ran through the pleasantries before turning to me and asking whether £10,000 would be considered enough to secure my future.

I nearly fell of the settee! I was only 16 and the prospect of earning that amount of money was mind-blowing.

Dario was also eager for me to move to digs nearer to Crewe. I don't think my parents were too keen on the idea and Paul suggested that the club could pay for me to have a car so I could commute instead.

Dario reacted in typically gruff fashion. I couldn't blame him really. I couldn't even drive at that point!

But Paul insisted, stating that I wasn't far away from 17 and would need a car once I had passed my test.

This time Dario responded with a knowing smile. He knew the game and eventually agreed that they would give me a substantial signing on fee that would enable me to pay for a car.

I chose a black MG metro and it gave me another means of transport to get to training.

I had been getting the train from the Port to Crewe every day along with another local lad called Maurice Doyle, so the car was a lifesaver.

Maurice was a top lad and we had a good laugh together. He was two years older than me so he was the one who drove it at first.

When I finally turned 17 he would sit in with me as I practiced. I think I owe him for that because it was his patience and advice that helped me to pass my test first time. He went on to play for QPR for a spell but the highlight of his career was probably a period at Millwall in the mid-90s.

With the YTS contract agreed, I was now a fully-fledged footballer and was all set to try and establish myself as a Gresty Road regular. I knew that Dario probably had other ideas but as the 88-89 campaign got underway an injury crisis meant he was forced to thrust the youngsters he was trying to protect back into action.

I was called upon to slot into the midfield and felt I did okay. I was doing a job for the team and helped us make an unbeaten start to the season ahead of a home clash with Darlington on September 17.

I had made my debut versus the Quakers just five months earlier and little did I know I would enjoy another day to remember on this occasion.

They too had a significant number of injuries in the lead up to the game and had even made a late plea to have it postponed, with their manager David Boon even attempting to get himself re-registered as a player in time for the encounter.

It didn't seem to affect them early on, however, and we were still defending for our lives when Ian Macowat managed to hack a Stonehouse shot off the line.

The ball was flicked on towards me and as I challenged one of their centre back's we both fell to the floor. I was first to my feet and began to lead the charge from the edge of the penalty area. I used my pace to surge forward, skipping beyond one defender and shimmying past a second before letting fly with a low drive that flashed into the back of the net.

It was my first goal in professional football and the Alex supporters later gave it the thumbs up by describing it as one of the best Gresty Road had seen in some time.

I didn't know what to do in celebration. In the end I just ran off! You'd think I'd have been shattered from my lung-bursting charge but the adrenalin just took over.

We went on to win the match 2-0 and my goal was the talk of the town for the next few days. Dario was delighted for me and told me to cherish the moment as I would remember it for the rest of my life.

He wasn't wrong about that. I can still remember every second of the build up to that goal.

I read a few days later that the boss had been overcome by the reaction of the crowd to my effort, describing the applause that went on way beyond the resultant kick off as 'one of the nicest things to have happened to me in my time in football."

When you consider what Dario has achieved in the game that is some accolade and something I am still very proud of to this day.

It was the first of two goals I scored during my time with Crewe. The other one was less spectacular. I just slotted the ball home from 10 yards during an entertaining 3-3 draw with Brentford.

The Darlington goal had inevitably propelled me into the spotlight and I continued to play regularly as we maintained our solid start to the season heading into the winter months.

Our youth team's cup run had seen many of England's elite clubs monitoring the progress of Gresty Road's youngsters and there was talk that Dario had received a 'name your price' offer for Steve Walters, who hadn't even featured for the first-team at that point.

Steve was regarded as one of the most talented youngsters in England and was a much sought after schoolboy international.

He'd been a star of the youth cup run and had played for the Three Lions at U15, U16 and U17 level having trained at Lilleshall. He went on to become the youngest ever player in Crewe's history at the end of that season. He seemed to have a golden future ahead of him.

I don't know why it didn't quite work out but it just goes to show the difference in level between youth football and a professional first-team. Your fast development can push you into the reckoning but once there you may not be ready.

Steve went on to play for Crewe for the next six years before carving out a career in non-league with the likes of Northwich Victoria and Morecambe.

It was around November that I was faced with a decision. Having been born in Wales I was eligible to play for them as well as England.

I had not rushed into a decision but always felt I would eventually end up playing for the country where I had grown up. The hospital where I was born was just over the Welsh border from my home in the Port. That was my only link to Wales.

On my 17th birthday I made my choice public after I had turned down the chance to join up with the Welsh squad for the European Youth Championships in Yugoslavia just a few weeks earlier.

Everything was clicking into place and I got the call for England U17s in a European Youth Championship game against France that was played at Bradford's Valley Parade ground. We drew 1-1 and I featured for 80 minutes before being substituted. Former Man United striker Andy Cole and ex-Spurs stopper Ian Walker were also in the team.

It was a great experience but maybe not as enjoyable as I would have imagined.

We played a long ball style that went against everything I had been taught at Crewe. Both myself and Steve (Walters) were used to the pass and move philosophy of Dario and co, so it was a bit of a culture shock. There was no way we would have rocked the boat though and just wanted to do our best for our country. It was an honour to be selected and every one of us gave our all when we pulled on the white shirt.

It wasn't long after that England display that I heard both Manchester United and Arsenal were keeping tabs on me. I felt like the world was at my feet.

That's when Dario's brilliant knack for keeping you focused came into play. As Crewe's injury problems began to clear up I was slowly eased out of regular action after featuring in 16 matches in the first half of the season.

The boss felt it would once again benefit my progress to have a break from the rigours of first-team football and I was sent back to play for the youth side again.

At the time I was exasperated by the decision but I got my head down and looked to work harder.

The coaching staff felt that I needed to improve my strength and I spent a lot of time in the remainder of that campaign hitting the weights in the gym.

After three months or so I started to notice a real difference and felt much stronger, particularly when running with the ball.

Being taken out of the limelight had knocked my confidence somewhat and I was struggling to hit the form that had earned me so many plaudits with the senior team.

If that wasn't bad enough, I then woke up one morning to see that my car had been vandalised with Tranmere Rovers slogans on the eve of a hugely significant match at Prenton Park.

It ended up costing hundreds of pounds to repair and the incident even made the local paper.

I spent the morning trying to wash away the vehicle primer they had used; hardly the ideal preparation for a game that would ultimately secure our promotion to division three. I ended up getting a lift to the ground to watch our lads claim the result that we needed.

We went on to finish third and while it was great to have played some role in that achievement the disappointment of the second part of the season meant I didn't enjoy it as much as I should have done.

The summer came and went but once again I fell short of pushing my way back into the first-team for our assault on the third division.

In fact, an incredible 75 matches elapsed until I finally returned to the line-up for an Easter Monday clash with Walsall. We won the match 3-1 and it felt great to get out there and play in front of that home crowd once again.

The club's record signing at the time, Darren Foreman hit a hat-trick to earn the points but I was surprised to hear the boss's praise heading in my direction during the post-match interviews.

He suggested that my display alongside Aidan Murphy was like having a 'new signing' and it did the world of good for my confidence to hear that he was pleased with my outing.

It gave me some momentum to build on and I played in most of the remaining matches that season.

I was now 18 and eager to cement a regular role. It was going to be a big pre-season for me.

I was still Crewe's Mr Versatile and began it at centre back. I remember losing a friendly 8-1 to Sheffield Wednesday but Dario insisted that none of the goals were down to me - not that it made me feel any better after enduring a 45 minute run around.

Despite the magnitude of the loss I managed to get a good write-up from the press against the Owls and the boss seemed pleased too. He felt it was a good learning experience for me and told the local newspaper that he was delighted by my attitude in training.

It was around this time that I decided to fly the nest and buy my first house. My parents had always been massively supportive but I was an adult now and I needed my space. It also helped to be a bit closer to the club's training ground.

We kicked off the season with a 1-1 draw at Fulham and I played as a sweeper. I enjoyed it and came off with a few pats on the back.

Things were starting to look up for me on a personal note but the team began to struggle in the league. Our only victory in our first eight matches came in a Rumbelows Cup clash against Grimsby Town. We managed to claim a 1-0 success to progress to the next round on the away goals rule following a 2-1 defeat in the first-leg.

It set up a second round draw that I had always dreamed of. We were paired with Liverpool.

I couldn't believe it. I was going to be facing players I still worshipped from the Kop. I couldn't make a regular pilgrimage to Anfield because of my commitments with Crewe but, when the fixture list allowed, I would savour my moments in L4.

We were expected to go there and be put to the sword. They were the reigning champions and had won their first six league games in the run-up to the first-leg.

We didn't have a prayer it seemed.

That proved to be the case too, but not before we gave them a bit of a scare.

On nine minutes we made a dream start when Andy Sussex tucked home the rebound after Craig Hignett's shot had rebounded back into his path.

We were the first team to take the lead against Liverpool that season and we gave a good account of ourselves throughout the encounter.

A lower league side scoring at Anfield can so often act as a red rag to a bull, particularly for a team managed by Kenny Dalglish and it wasn't long before they responded.

Dean Greygoose was in goal for us and he had a blinder despite being on the receiving end of a 5-1 defeat. He kept out a John Barnes penalty and produced a string of top-drawer saves that quite rightly had many hailing him as our man of the match.

We were fortunate to have the experienced head of Kenny Swain at the back and he was a constant source of reassurance as we fought to keep the Reds from running riot.

We managed to keep the score down for over two thirds of the contest. It was still 2-1 up until the 69th minute when Ray Houghton rifled a shot in off the upright. Ian Rush then added a late double to rub salt in our wounds.

As I trudged off the pitch at the final whistle I couldn't help but glance around at a half-full Anfield and wonder what it would be like to play here week in, week out in front of a sell-out crowd.

I made a pledge to myself that this wouldn't be the last time I would get to play on the famous turf.

There had been a lot of newspaper talk about Liverpool's search for a right-back and following that game I was cited as a potential target alongside the likes of Oldham's Earl Barrett and Paul Warhurst.

It was a great feeling to see my name in the same sentence as my boyhood heroes but I knew it was just speculation.

We would go on to lose the second-leg 4-1 at Gresty Road and although my stock continued to soar it was a disappointing season overall.

We struggled throughout a tough third division campaign.

I struck the second goal of my professional career in a 3-3 draw with Brentford but it was a rare moment of joy as we were relegated back to the league's bottom tier.

A 3-0 win at home to Mansfield Town on the final day did little to banish the feeling that we could have done better and with the prospect of playing at a lower level again, my dream of a return to Anfield seemed even further away.

Little did I know it was a reality that lay just around the corner.

CHAPTER FOUR

The newspapers dropped to the table with a thud.

I peered over the pile that almost reached halfway to the ceiling to see Paul's excited expression.

He had made an early morning dash to the newsagents and bought every publication he could get his hands on so he could bring them over to my house.

The result of his endeavours was now towering over my breakfast plate, tempting me to see what had been written about Liverpool's new rookie full-back.

Our clash at Manchester United appeared to have enjoyed a clean sweep of the back pages.

A quick flick through some of the tabloids informed me that my performance had been given the thumbs-up.

I was beaming from ear to ear as I read some of the more generous copy. It was a nice feeling, but I knew there was no time to revel in the glory. Anfield was calling.

I'd almost fainted when Ronnie Moran told us to report for training as usual as we had gone our separate ways after the match.

The exhaustion must have been written all over my face because Deano patted me on the back and told me not to worry. It was just going to be a bath.

A bath?

It sounded a bit weird to me. But who was I to question Liverpool FC's methods?

My body was still aching as I polished off the remnants of my toast. I was just glad it wasn't going to be a full-on session.

I said my farewells to Paul and rather gingerly made my way to the car.

I relived the previous day's action in my head. I still couldn't quite comprehend what had happened to me.

I have to admit I felt a bit awkward heading straight for Anfield's dressing room bath. I was still a complete newcomer and there I was going 'el bollocko' with my heroes.

As I sat there, next to some of the finest players to have ever worn the red shirt, I was still pinching myself. It still felt like a dream. I'd played for Liverpool in one of the biggest games in English football's calendar and managed to hold my own.

I later realised that the bath was Ronnie and Roy's way of checking on the players to make sure we hadn't gone out and got completely wasted after the match.

It actually did me the world of good and when I finally got out my muscles felt less fatigued.

It proved to be a whirlwind first week at Liverpool and it was perhaps unsurprising that there was an increased level of interest in me.

I was desperate to have the opportunity to hold down my place in the side, but I knew circumstances would leave me chomping at the bit.

I was cup-tied for the League Cup win at Stoke City so there was a bit of a break between the United clash and my next game for the Reds at Chelsea.

It was an international week and most of our lads were away with their respective countries. I was one of a handful of players left behind and the backroom staff decided I should have a run out for the reserves at Anfield.

Phil Thompson was the manager and they were trying out five at the back, a system we would come to use in later years.

The way I had been taught at Crewe was that if you played that formation, and were in the wing back position, you would always stay behind and mark the winger.

But Liverpool's style was to stand in front of him. I couldn't adapt to that at first because it felt unnatural to have the attacker behind me. Every time the ball was fired down my flank Thommo would scream at me. You name the swear word, he shouted it!

Different managers have different ideas. As far as I was concerned I was a defender and if the ball went over my head, I would have to rely on the right centre back to come across and sweep up. If he doesn't, then you look stupid. It just didn't feel right to me and it was reflected in my performance.

I shuffled into the dressing room at the interval and was immediately slaughtered by Thompson. It wasn't a subtle bollocking either. He did it in front of *everyone*.

I noticed that Souness was an interested observer so I decided I had better stick up for myself and explain.

My argument fell on deaf ears and after some more stern words I was simply told to stick to the tactics being deployed.

In the second half I did what they said but I don't think it worked because it was very new to all of us.

Despite the issues of that encounter it was a proud moment for me to pull on the red of Liverpool at Anfield for the first time. It may have only been a second-string run-out but I was still overjoyed.

It made me even more eager to sample the atmosphere generated by a packed Kop in full cry.

There were 20 days between my appearance at Old Trafford and a home clash with Coventry City. It felt like an eternity.

I was missing out on the League Cup and had not been registered in time to play in the early rounds of the UEFA Cup either. It was frustrating, particularly as I had done so well against United. I wanted to try and maintain that momentum.

When I did finally get out onto that pitch the nerves were well and truly jangling again. The sight of the Kop made my mouth dry and I just wanted the game to get underway so I could focus on the task in hand.

Ask any player and they will tell you about the importance of a good first touch.

That didn't happen.

We'd just kicked off and the ball found its way back to Bruce Grobbelaar. He rolled it out to me and I moved forward towards the halfway line. I tried to lay a pass infield to one of our midfielders but it was intercepted. David Smith picked up possession and he must've thought Christmas had come early because he was suddenly presented with a clear run at goal.

I surged through the gears and ate up the ground. Just as he was about to let fly I managed to slide in to produce a timely block and avert the danger. They appealed for a penalty but I definitely got the ball. I puffed out my cheeks and looked at Brucie.

He shrugged and bowled the ball out to the opposite flank. I breathed a huge sigh of relief.

Later, Ronnie Moran gave Brucie a right earful for putting me under pressure. He thought it was a stupid thing to do to someone who was making their home bow. I thought it was a bit unfair. I think he was just trying to help settle my nerves by giving me an early touch.

I can only imagine what would have happened had they scored from my error. I've no doubt that I would have ended up being hauled off at half-time. I would have gone to pieces.

Aside from that brief flirtation with disaster, I put in a solid shift and we ended up winning 1-0 thanks to a Ray Houghton goal just after the half hour mark.

I enjoyed playing with Ray. His experience had been vital against United. We worked well together.

I don't think he really got the credit he deserved for what he did at Liverpool. I certainly think we sold him too early. He left at the end of the season and had a major impact at Aston Villa. He went on to have a long career, playing well into his late 30s. He famously scored the winner against Italy when he was representing the Republic of Ireland at the 1994 World Cup.

It was a short-lived partnership but one that I relished nonetheless. He always tucked in when I bombed forward and that prevented us from losing our shape. I suppose I did the running for us down that right flank but when you play with someone of Ray's quality, it always makes your job easier.

He had a fabulous season and was amongst the PFA player of the year contenders. He scored 12 goals from midfield and was Mr consistency at a time when the squad was struggling with injuries. Gary Pallister went on to win it but if I'd had my way, I'd have given it to Ray.

I was in and out of the side for the next few months, but when I was called upon, I produced some fine displays. I soon settled into my new life as a Liverpool player.

On the day I had signed, Souness had told me they would re-evaluate my contract if I played 10 matches. He also said he'd throw in a car.

After 12 games I wondered what I should do. I went and knocked on his door.

- Excuse me, Mr Souness. When I signed you told me to speak to you when I played 10 games and that you'd give me a pay rise and a car. Well, I've played 12 now…

He looked at me with a wry smile.

- I'll tell you what Rob. Play another 10 and we'll see.

It's funny looking back on that now. I felt a bit embarrassed to have asked the question in the end.

I don't think he'd envisaged me playing 10 games so quickly. I'd only been there a couple of months and maybe he was making sure I wasn't just a flash in the pan.

By the time I'd reached his next target I'd featured for England's senior side. This time I was rewarded and I was offered a new contract that took me up to £2,500 per week.

I never did get the car.

So Graeme, if you're reading this, you still owe me one!

I was living the dream but it wasn't without the odd rueful moment.

As I've mentioned, the club had already registered their squad for the first few rounds of the UEFA Cup by the time I joined from Crewe. It meant I was forced to watch one of the games of the season from the stands.

We took on Auxerre in the second round and were faced with a mountain to climb. We had lost the first-leg 2-0 in France and needed a minor miracle to progress.

It was the type of occasion that Liverpool had become famous for; an improbable task that left many observers writing our European obituary.

They should have known better.

Roared on by a packed Anfield crowd, we took an early lead through Jan Molby's penalty.

You could see the belief ignite in the eyes of those wearing red as fear began to creep into the French side's play.

Ironically, it was our right-back that drew us level on aggregate on the half hour mark. Mike Marsh was a versatile midfielder who had been filling in during my absence and it was he who arrived late in the box to nod home a superb far post header.

It was the sort of night that had been missing in L4 for far too long and I can recall the hair rising on the back of my neck with the intensity of the atmosphere.

As the clock ticked down it was all set for someone to emerge as the hero of the hour and I was delighted that my first ever Liverpool roommate was the man who stepped up to the plate.

Wally Walters was a talented winger with a penchant for overdoing stepovers, but he was also a match winner on his day. That night was one of the finest moments of his Reds career as he sealed a stunning 3-0 success by calmly steering a shot into the Kop end net.

It was a game that lingered long in my memory. For most clubs it would go down as one of their greatest-ever European nights, but when you are Liverpool it barely makes the top 20.

It was hard not to get caught up in the elation of the dressing room. I was delighted for the lads and pleased we had made it through to the next round. I just wished I'd been able to play. It felt incredible in the stand so I can only imagine what it was like out on the pitch.

It was a minor frustration. I would have been daft not to realise that the last few months of 1991 had been very kind to me. The start of 1992 brought with it a whole host of nice surprises too.

First up we faced a trip to my old stomping ground after we were drawn to face Crewe in the third round of the FA Cup at Gresty Road.

You couldn't have scripted it could you? Less than three months after swapping the Alex for Anfield I was heading back to my roots.

It was exciting.

I saw it as a great opportunity to say goodbye to the fans. I'd literally gone overnight so it was great to see them again.

It's such a small, friendly club. They love to see their past players moving up the football ladder. It's a source of pride that they are able to nurture starlets who go on and have a big impact at the top level of the English game.

It was all so familiar for me. The narrow corridors and the small, pokey dressing rooms. It had been my home for so many years and it still felt that way.

The household names of Liverpool were the star attraction wherever they went so it came as a bit of a surprise that so much of the attention was on me.

I think the Crewe staff, their players and the fans were just all really pleased for me. They all wanted to shake my hand and share a joke. It was a warm reception and the banter was as good as ever. It was almost a shame that there was a game to play at the end of it all.

But once you cross that white line sentiment goes out of the window and I think we were very professional that night. We eased to a 4-0 win and I had a hand in two of the goals.

I created the opener for Steve McManaman on 10 minutes before John Barnes's quick-fire double crushed Crewe's hopes of an upset. One was a particularly classy back heel that had all corners of the ground rising to their feet in applause.

Barnesy then put the seal on the victory with his hat-trick from the spot after Dave McKearney had brought my surging run to an abrupt halt late on.

Barnesy had only just returned from a serious Achilles injury so it was nice that he capped his comeback by picking up the match ball. It was a reminder of what we had been missing and illustrated once again what a sensational player he was on his day.

A lot of Liverpool fans have reminded me about that occasion over the years and some have even suggested that I should have taken the penalty.

It never even entered my head. For a start, I don't know how I would have felt scoring against Crewe and let's face it, there were probably eight or nine other players ahead of me in the queue!

The next few games saw us continue our good form and a 2-0 success over reigning champions Arsenal on a flood-lit night at Anfield moved us up to third, eight points adrift of leaders Manchester United.

Murmurs of a title challenge began to creep into the dressing room chat but that was swiftly ended just three days later when we suffered a shock 2-1 home defeat against Chelsea.

I think you know it's not going to be your day when Vinnie Jones scores a stunning volley at the Kop end. He was hardly renowned for his technique but we can't use that as an excuse. We didn't perform to our usual level and got what we deserved.

Maybe it was the curse of the manager of the month award. Souness had received the gong for January prior to kick off. He probably stuck it in the bin on the way home!

To top it off we suffered some serious knocks to key personnel in that game and the next few weeks were disastrous for any lingering hopes we had of landing the title.

Barnesy, Michael Thomas, Nicol, Molby and Nick Tanner all picked up injuries and our results inevitably suffered.

Quite a few of the lads seemed to be having problems with their left Achilles. It was very strange to see so many professionals struck down with exactly the same issue. We all began to wonder if it was something to do with the training.

Souness's detractors had a field day. They blamed his methods and insisted that he and his assistant, Phil Boersma would need to radically change their approach. The suggestion was that Liverpool had not endured such a lengthy injury list prior to their arrival.

I can see where the critics were coming from, but it had nothing to do with Graeme or Phil.

Ronnie Moran was the one who took the majority of the sessions. He'd done that before Graeme came in and after he left too. So it was wrong to blame Souness.

We had no explanation for it. It was just one of those things. We tried anything in the end.

For example, we used to do a long run every day in training. We always ran in the same direction and thought nothing of it until over half a dozen of us were crocked.

So the following week we started jogging the opposite way. It was all psychological.

Many people were writing us off but we were still in the FA Cup and felt we still had a team to match anyone on our day.

We seemed intent on doing it the hard way though. We needed an Anfield replay to see off a dogged Bristol Rovers in round four and were faced with the same scenario in the following tie against Ipswich Town.

It was a windswept affair down at Portman Road and they were the better side for large chunks of the encounter.

We were just pleased to get them back to Anfield where we survived another rollercoaster evening to triumph 3-2 after extra time.

We'd been drawn away to lower division sides in the first three rounds of the cup and were relieved to finally get a home tie when we were paired with Aston Villa in the quarter-finals.

It was a tough game and came just four days after the disappointment of being knocked out of the UEFA Cup by Genoa. We were acutely aware that it was win or bust.

We had been fielding patched up sides for a number of matches but received some good news when Thomas declared himself fit after missing six weeks through injury.

Many fans had been shocked by Souness's decision to bring him to Liverpool. It was highly controversial, particularly as he had been the man who scored the Arsenal goal that killed our hopes of securing the double in 1989.

His stoppage time winner had given the Gunners the 2-0 win they had needed to clinch the title at Anfield and for a lot of supporters he had a bit of making up to do - and that included me!

He went some way to doing it though, when he got the only goal of the game against the Villans. It was a superb run from midfield that broke the offside trap and a stylish finish at the Kop end. It was also his first goal at Anfield since that infamous day.

I also came out of the game with a fair bit of credit. Souness had switched me to left-back to combat the pace of Tony Daley. He was a real whippet and there were few players as quick as him in the league. It didn't concern me as I had yet to meet a player who could blow me away for pace and I felt I did a pretty good job of marking him out of the game.

I was desperate to see which team we would face in the last four.

We were so close to Wembley now and I had started to pick up the scent.

I was driving home when the draw was made. I think I even missed my turn off the motorway because I was listening to the radio so intently.

- And Liverpool will face.... Portsmouth.

I beeped the horn in delight and punched the air.

Jim Smith's side were just off the play-offs in the old second division and we would be heading into the clash as strong favourites.

You can never take anything for granted in football, particularly in cup competitions and I was about to learn that the hard way.

We were warned about complacency throughout the week leading up to the game. Pompey had looked strong in the cup and had some talented youngsters in the shape of Kit Symons and Darren Anderton.

On a sweltering day at Arsenal's old Highbury ground, it was the latter who looked to have dashed our hopes of FA Cup glory when he broke the deadlock to fire Pompey ahead in extra-time.

As he celebrated in front of the Pompey fans, I looked around at my teammates and could see there was very little left in the tank.

We seemed down and out.

We needed some inspiration but no-one looked capable of producing a moment of magic.

But then we got a lifeline.

We were awarded a free-kick in a dangerous position on the edge of the penalty area with just four minutes left.

Barnesy stepped up and assessed the situation. It was a huge moment and I became acutely aware of how quiet it had gone in the stadium.

I glanced towards the Liverpool fans and clocked a couple who had their eyes closed. Their hands were pressed together in a form of prayer.

Inside, I was doing the same.

If there was one player who could pull Liverpool out of the mire back then, it was Barnesy.

I recalled a free-kick he had scored against Arsenal a few years earlier and urged him to repeat it under my breath.

- Come on Barnesy...

The roar broke the silence as he curled a shot over the wall and beyond the keeper.

It was in! We were level and we were all going mental. We were convinced he'd restored parity.

Barnesy was jumping in the air, screaming 'Yes'!

We didn't realise that it had cannoned back off the post. Thank god Ronnie Whelan had stayed alert enough to follow it in and force the ball over the line.

We all went mental. Again.

We didn't say it afterwards but we had all felt it was over until that moment.

We'd survived a huge scare and I became even more convinced our name was on the cup.

Of course, we still had the small matter of a replay to look forward to and we soon found out that we would be going into that *without* our manager.

We'd left Highbury on the team coach as normal. It had been a long day and we were all relatively happy to still be in the competition.

I was planning on getting a few hours sleep until we were told we were going to stop off at a hotel for a few beers first.

The alarm bells immediately began to ring in my head. That was something we never did.

When we arrived at our destination Graeme took us into a private room and bought us all a drink.

My granddad Bill teaching Declan some skills

My first visit to Anfield

My first taste of silverware

Do you think I could get those shorts any higher?

In Jersey with my dad Pete

My first trip to Wembley

Out and about with my sister Kate and my mum Joan

Me and my dad Paul in Spain

Me and my granddad posing for the camera

My Crewe debut aged just 16

My first day at Liverpool

Those infamous white suits

FA Cup winners

Open top bus ride with the lads

Coca Cola Cup Winners

Another nearly moment in front of goal!

Toasting our Coca Cola Cup success with Babbsy and Scalesy

Sharing a joke with the club doctor (Mark Waller),
a man I spent a lot of time with!

On my Stag do with Mark Wrig

Sue and I on our wedding day celebrating with the lads

Once he was sure he had everyone's attention he told us he had something he needed to say. I could feel the dread growing in the pit of my stomach.

I could tell by his expression something was wrong. He took a deep breath and then dropped the bombshell.

He had a heart problem and needed to have a major operation to save his life.

The silence was deafening.

He maintained his composure and tried to remain upbeat.

He said that it just meant he wouldn't be involved for a while and that Ronnie Moran and Roy Evans would take over. He finished by wishing us all good luck.

We were stunned. No-one spoke. We just looked at each other in silence.

A few of the lads finally followed Souness out of the room and offered him their best wishes. Others started to talk amongst themselves.

The overriding feeling as we got back on the coach was that we were going to win this cup.

Yes, some of us may not have seen eye to eye with him, but when it comes to matters of life or death, it gives you a clear perspective on things.

We were going to win it and we were going to win it for the boss.

We had just under two weeks to get ourselves ready for the replay at Villa Park. We warmed up for it by losing both of our league games; at home to Wimbledon and, ironically, away to Aston Villa. It was clear we were concentrating all of our energy on Portsmouth.

We had quite a strong line-up for our biggest game of the season to-date and went about our pre-match preparations in confident mood.

Souness was watching it via satellite at a hospital in Manchester and we wanted to give him a comfortable evening.

Pompey had other ideas.

Once again they raised their game and gave us a torrid night.

They should have been ahead inside the opening quarter of an hour but Anderton lobbed wide of the post after Brucie had completely misjudged a long ball over the top.

We were struggling to create any openings and should have been dumped out of the cup late on when Alan McLoughlin smashed a close range shot against the crossbar.

Once more relief swept over my body.

The tension continued to grow and extra-time passed by in a blur.

With three minutes left until penalties Ronnie and Roy made the decision to replace me with Mark Walters. It was good management. I wasn't comfortable with the responsibility of a spot-kick and Wally was an experienced lad who could well have taken one had we needed him.

As it turned out, we didn't.

After such a spirited display, Portsmouth lost their nerve in what was the first-ever shoot-out to decide a place at Wembley. Martin Kuhl, Warren Neill and John Beresford all failed to convert.

Barnesy, Rushie and Deano netted for us to ensure we were on our way to Wembley for the fourth time in six years.

It was an incredible feeling. My first season with the club and it was going to conclude with an FA Cup final appearance.

The euphoria of that success did little for our league form. We were pretty useless in the final few matches and won just one of our last seven outings.

That did happen to be a notable 2-0 success against Manchester United at Anfield. It was a win that denied them the title and handed it to Leeds.

It was an enjoyable occasion.

We went ahead through Rushie, who fired home his first ever goal against our fierce rivals. He was such an incredible goalscorer that it had always surprised me he had never found the net in those titanic encounters. It was a stat that United fans would often take great glee in relaying in the build up to matches. It was now one that Rushie had rammed back down their throats.

We played some superb football that afternoon. I was enjoying getting forward at every opportunity and got a bit carried away when I hammered a shot that almost flew out of the ground!

The match was live on ITV and Paul recorded it for me. When I watched it back I had to laugh at my rush of blood.

The late Brian Moore was the commentator for the game and he summed it up perfectly.

- Rob Jones...ohhhh... he's never scored for Liverpool and with shooting like that, he never will."

Little did he know how right he would be!

We were by far and away the better side that day and it was no more than we deserved when Walters wrapped up the points late on.

I remember the Kop rubbing salt in United's wounds by singing 'Always look on the bright side of life', a song that had been a favourite for their fans over the course of the season. It was a great way to finish off our home campaign.

A goalless draw at Sheffield Wednesday set us up for Wembley, but I wasn't involved that afternoon.

I'd started to feel intense pain in my shins in the hours following the United clash and ended up resting right up until the day before the final. At one point I feared missing out on the biggest game of my life. It wasn't a nice feeling and I was relieved when I was given the okay to play.

Sunderland were massive underdogs. They were another side struggling in the old second division, but we weren't going to be taking anything for granted. We'd seen how tough the semi-final had been with Portsmouth and we were expecting them to follow Pompey's example.

I wasn't particularly nervous. I'd played at Wembley just a few months earlier with England so I was more excited than anything else.

It had been a tough season for everyone associated with the club and a trophy would certainly round everything off in a positive fashion.

I had always looked forward to cup final day as a kid. I loved watching the big build up on television and savoured every moment.

I expected the same sensations as a player, but to be honest, it all passed by in a blur. The bus ride from Sopwell House hotel to the ground and the walk on the pitch all went far too fast.

Before I knew it I was in the dressing room waiting impatiently for the referee to call us out into the tunnel.

I thought about my family watching proudly from the stands and recalled my first trip to the famous old stadium; the 1986 all-Merseyside affair against Everton.

Tickets were like gold dust but my granddad had managed to swing us a pair thanks to a phone call he made to Geoff Twentyman.

He insisted upon paying for them himself and told Paul to take me down to Wembley as his treat.

It was a brilliant gesture and set up what was a wonderful day.

At half-time it looked like we may end up disappointed but a fabulous second-half revival saw us go on to lift the cup courtesy of a 3-1 success.

I remembered that big Jan Molby had a stormer that day and glanced over to the great Dane sitting in quiet contemplation. Once again the enormity of my rapid rise over the past eight months hit home.

Back in '86 I was in the stands hailing his huge impact. Now I would be standing shoulder to shoulder with him on the pitch.

Paul and I had been in joyous mood in the aftermath of our victory over Everton. We'd seen our team make history as King Kenny's reds clinched the double. The stream of incessant red filing out of the stadium was carried along by the soundtrack of You'll Never Walk Alone.

It should have been one of the high points of the day but proved to be one that haunted me for some weeks after.

We were distracted by the jubilant songs and excited chatter about the game and didn't realised that we had been forced towards a solitary exit before it was too late.

There were usually two ways you could go but for some reason the police had blocked one of them. It meant all of the fans were funnelled down this one way.

I can tell you now, I shit myself.

I was squashed up against some lads in front of us and I could tell by Paul's face he was worried. The police horses were pushing everyone and it was getting to the stage where it was difficult to breath.

I was close to dropping to the ground when Paul managed to pick me up and lift me on to a nearby wall. I was relieved to be out of it but he was still trapped.

Everyone was going mad. It was ridiculous that we were being forced into this situation.

I don't know if another exit was opened or how they resolved the situation, but just when it seemed there would be nowhere to go, the pressure began to subside.

Eventually you could see a bit of space between each supporter and Paul was able to break free and take me off the wall.

We walked in silence. It had been a truly frightening experience and the triumphant mood had fallen flat. As we began the long drive home, we were just pleased to have made it out safely.

It was a moment that drifted to the back of my subconscious until an FA Cup semi-final in April 1989.

One of the darkest afternoons in English football's history.

It was a huge tragedy and one that the authorities should have been held accountable for from the start. Instead, they lay blame elsewhere.

It has been such a long time in coming, but finally the truth has emerged.

It took an incredible 23 years.

23 years of lies and setbacks. But the families maintained their dignity throughout. Now it is only a matter of time until justice prevails too.

No-one should lose their life at a football match.

The 96 and my own personal experience in 1986 were my last thoughts when we finally got the call.

Ronnie Moran led us into the tunnel and then out onto the pitch. He was flanked by Sunderland's caretaker manager Malcolm Crosby.

I know Ronnie was incredibly proud to have that honour. He was the one you'd hear barking orders at you throughout games, but he was surprisingly quiet that afternoon. Maybe it was the emotion or the fact he was effectively the manager and took a more pensive approach.

It wasn't as if he hadn't been there before though! He'd been part of all of Liverpool's successes since the days of Bill Shankly.

We also had a wealth of players used to winning trophies.

When you consider all of those factors, I suppose it didn't harm us too much that Souness wasn't in charge for the game.

It says a lot about the strength of the man's character that he had insisted he was in attendance.

The specialists had relented and allowed him to attend the match accompanied by our club doctor, Bill Reid.

A lot has been said about Souness and his time as manager but he cared deeply about trying to ensure the club was successful. He felt by being there he could help in some way, even if it was detrimental to his health. You cannot knock that level of commitment.

I think Souness being there gave everyone a boost. I'm not sure how much he had to do with picking the team but the main thing was that we won the match.

We didn't play that well in the first half and I don't think we could have had too many complaints if Sunderland had gone in ahead at the interval.

They had a player called John Byrne who had scored in every round. He was their main danger man and he had a glorious chance to get them off to a dream start inside 15 minutes.

A left-wing corner was flicked into his path just inside the six-yard box but he snatched at it and fired his shot by the post.

People have since told me that I was lucky to get away with a foul on Peter Davenport in that first period. They have insisted Sunderland should have had a penalty. I've even read it in an old newspaper cutting I have from the game. To be honest I can't recall the incident.

I can vividly remember the mistake I made in the opening moments of my Anfield debut against Coventry, but not that one. So my response is always the same. It couldn't have been that clear-cut if I have no recollection of it.

Sunderland had enjoyed a good spell but they didn't make the most of it and I think our experience told in the end.

A significant moment was when we moved Macca onto the right. He'd had a relatively quiet first half by his standards, which was perhaps understandable given that it was his first game in a month following a cartilage injury sustained in the semi-final with Portsmouth.

Judging by his display after the interval, he had just needed time to get into his groove. He tore them to shreds and was later named man of the match.

Within moments of the restart he had created the opener. He jinked past a couple of defenders and angled a great ball into the area for Thomas. He allowed the ball to run across his body before crashing a stunning volley back across goal and into the top corner.

It was a fantastic goal. For some reason it isn't one that people pick out as a particularly memorable strike, but I think it should be up there when you consider great cup final goals.

That effort gave us the platform to step up our performance and I don't think there was ever a doubt over whether we'd go on to win it.

We had some experienced heads in there with the likes of Wrighty, Steve Nicol and, of course, Rushie.

Rushie was the man who got our all-important second goal, an effort that saw him become the all-time record scorer in FA Cup finals with five to his name.

Thomas was again involved, providing the pass for Saunders to tee up his compatriot to fire home.

That clinched the victory and I made sure I was right in the middle of the celebrations at the final whistle. It had been a hard season for everyone. We'd had issues both on and off the pitch, but we had ended it on a high.

I remember Wrighty heading up the steps to lift the trophy. He received it from the Duke and Duchess of Kent before bellowing the immortal words 'you fucking beauty!'

I was a few players back in the queue and didn't hear him do it. He took a bit of stick for that but it was just pure elation. It had been a difficult first year in red for him but there he was lifting the FA Cup as Liverpool captain. That was why he had moved to Anfield after all, to win silverware. He apologised profusely and I think the royals understood it was down to unbridled joy.

It was a fabulous feeling climbing those steps. I had been a lower league footballer just a few months earlier and I'd been in the crowd as a spectator for the previous year's clash between Crystal Palace and Manchester United.

Dario had received 12 tickets for the final and asked if any of us fancied it. I thought it would be nice to go along and watch. Obviously I was hoping Palace would win! It finished 3-3 and I thought they were really unlucky. Ian Wright scored two that day but they eventually lost the replay 1-0.

So to be involved as a player, a year on was incredible.

It felt like an age waiting for the cup to be passed down to me. When it finally arrived it was everything I hoped it would be.

I was an FA Cup winner with Liverpool FC. It didn't get much better than that. I gave the pristine piece of silver a quick kiss and passed it on with the promise we would reacquaint ourselves later.

I made my way further down the line and was presented with my medal. I didn't even notice it was the wrong one!

Sunderland had gone up first and been handed the winners' medals by mistake. It meant I was celebrating on the pitch with a losers' medal hanging around my neck.

It mattered little. By now, we were in full celebration mode and doing a lap of the Wembley pitch.

Souness looked tired and frail but it was great to see him take the trophy off big Jan for the briefest of moments.

He pressed his lips to it tenderly and shared a quiet moment with his first trophy as Liverpool boss before handing it back to the rest of us.

Bill Reid was still by his side and had frequently reminded the boss throughout the game not to get too excited. When he did seem to be getting too involved, Bill was there to squeeze his shoulder and warn him with a stern look.

It meant he was missing from the night of celebrations and it was probably wise. We didn't hold back and a lot of it is rather hazy!

I vaguely recall Phil Thompson dropping the cup and putting a big dent in the lid. It could have been anyone though. If they'd blamed me the next day I'd have probably believed it. To put it simply, I made sure I thoroughly enjoyed the occasion.

As had become his custom, Paul bought all of the newspapers the following day.

When I finally got around to reading them, I was delighted to see the Scottish Sunday Post had actually given me their man of the match award.

It made me laugh because it said: 'Born in Wales, plays for England. What a pity he didn't have a Scottish granny!'

I was due to meet up with England in the immediate aftermath of our victory. Had the FA insisted then Wrighty and I would have missed out on the open top bus parade around Liverpool.

We were both desperate to tour the city with the team and got a lot of criticism for making that decision.

Thankfully, it all blew over and it was all set up for me to conclude a fairytale first season in the topflight by playing for England at Euro 92.

Unfortunately, a problem with my shins that I had been nursing for the previous month or so would rule me out. It was a bitter blow after such a sensational start to life at Anfield.

I tried not to let it get me down. There would surely be more tournaments to come in the years ahead, wouldn't there?

CHAPTER FIVE

Six hundred and eighty-two minutes.

That was the sum total of my England career.

Eight caps over an injury-plagued period of three years and thirty-seven days.

I'm proud to have represented my country at the highest level but must admit part of me does feel I could have done so much more on the international stage.

My last cap came in a goalless draw with Greece in March 1995. I was just 23 and looking forward to a long and distinguished career with the Three Lions.

Terry Venables had taken over the hot-seat from Graham Taylor and in his first seven matches in charge I had started six of them. I was recognised as England's number one, number two so to speak. Gary Neville was emerging at Manchester United but he was playing second fiddle to me at that point.

The only match that I did miss in that period was a friendly encounter against the Republic of Ireland. The game was actually abandoned at half-time but the reason I wasn't involved was because Liverpool were taking on Crystal Palace in the Coca Cola Cup semi-final first-leg on the same night.

It gave Venables the chance to have a look at Wimbledon's Warren Barton but after Ireland went ahead through David Kelly, the match was abandoned on 27 minutes as a result of crowd trouble.

It's easy for me to sit here now and say that if injuries hadn't hampered my involvement I would have gone on to play over 50 times for England. Who knows, maybe I would have. It's easy to play the 'if' game.

It had all started so well for me too.

I was in the midst of my first season at Liverpool and we had just drawn 1-1 away to Bristol Rovers in the fourth round of the FA Cup.

I was expecting a little break with the internationals coming up. I wasn't even thinking about England and was contemplating a short break abroad when I was stopped by a couple of reporters at the Melwood gates.

They asked me if I'd be looking out for the squad when it was revealed the following day and I have to be honest, my initial reaction was to laugh out loud. I hadn't even been aware that it was about to be named by Graham Taylor.

They must have had some inkling anyway because on the day that it was announced they were all gathered outside Anfield.

We were getting changed after training and the club secretary, Peter Robinson came up to me and told me he had received a fax.

I had been named in the squad.

I was completely shell-shocked and wary of all the attention that my inclusion would create. After all, I'd been a fourth division player just four months ago. The media love all those rags to riches type of stories so I actually greeted the news with a mix of joy and apprehension.

Deano must have sensed that something wasn't right. He suggested I go home with him to avoid any press who might decide to follow me back to my house for a quote.

I didn't want any fuss so I just agreed. We got in his car and I hid as we made a speedy getaway. We played a bit of tennis at his house and were quite happy relaxing. What we didn't know at the time was that the press were ringing everyone they could think of in an attempt to track me down.

When I look back it was probably a bit stupid. I know Deano meant well and he was only looking out for me, but in hindsight I should have just gone out and spoken to them for five minutes after training. Maybe I got on the wrong side of some of them that day by doing that. I was young and hadn't been under such an intense spotlight before. It's not something I have a deep regret about but I do think I could have saved myself a whole lot of hassle that day.

Eventually Deano started getting calls.

We knew it couldn't go on, so he relented and revealed that I was laying low at his house. Before we knew it the Press had arrived from London.

It wasn't too taxing. They took some pictures of me with an England cap and got a quick quote. It wasn't the grilling I was anticipating.

I suppose it's proof that it really doesn't matter how young you are. If you are playing regularly and doing well for a top team like Liverpool, then England are going to look at you.

Taylor must have seen something in me and decided that he needed to have a closer look in his England set-up.

Lee Dixon and Paul Parker were both vying for the right-back berth around that time and I would be challenging them for a place in the team.

You can't really get much bigger than Liverpool and the players we have, but I was still a bit star struck when I joined up with the squad and I began chatting to people like Gary Lineker and Paul Gascoigne. They had made a huge impact at World Cup Italia 90, a tournament that really caught the imagination and helped change the landscape of football forever.

The game I got the call for was a friendly with France at Wembley. Alan Shearer was also in the squad that day and he would go on to make his debut alongside me.

Initially, Taylor was going to select the late David Rocastle at right-wing back. They actually played the team in training and it included three at the back with the two wing-backs.

But Rocastle got a kick on his ankle a couple of days before the match and it swelled up. It opened the door for me to come into the side and I made my bow on February 19, 1992 in a 2-0 win.

Shearer marked his big night with a goal while Lineker came off the bench to net the other. Mark Wright played on the right side of the defence and that was good for me because there was a bit of an understanding there from playing together at Liverpool. It was possibly a reason why Taylor opted to throw me in too.

Michel Platini's side hadn't lost a match in two years so it was all the more impressive that we turned them over. They had the likes of Eric

Cantona, Jean-Pierre Papin and Didier Deschamps in their side and they were a quality outfit.

It was another eye opener for me. Less than six months earlier I'd been sitting in the Crewe dressing room preparing to run out at Gresty Road and now here I was rubbing shoulders with England's finest.

Of course, it wasn't my first match in an England shirt. I had represented the Three Lions at U18 level back in my Crewe days.

I remember one occasion in particular. We were playing a game against Greece in Athens. It was a sweltering day and we knew it was going to be an occasion where we would need plenty of water on the touchline.

The Greeks were clearly eager to exploit this. We were just about to start our warm up on the pitch when we realised they had locked us in the dressing room.

It was ridiculously hot in there. We were banging on the door desperate to get out. It was like a sauna. You don't expect things like that to happen at international level but they seemed intent on trying anything to gain the advantage.

As it happened, we went on to win the game and I played right midfield.

It was a moment that struck a chord with me though and I realised that I needed to be prepared for anything. It's something that I think helped me in my preparations for my senior bow.

I found out I was in the team the night before the match.

I was sitting opposite Lineker eating the evening meal when Taylor came over and said two simple but mind-blowing words. 'You're in.'

The next 24 hours were a whirlwind but I always recall a moment in the dressing room prior to kick off. The late Alan Ball, an England great in his own right, came over and told me to go out there and just enjoy my football. I thought that was a nice touch and it really helped to settle some of the butterflies flapping about in the pit of my stomach.

There was also a telegram that had arrived from Italy courtesy of David Platt.

It read: 'Don't worry, it's just like Crewe.'

It made me chuckle and relieved some of the tension. I'd been aware of Platty at Crewe and we had spoken but he had moved on to bigger things by the time I finally made it into the first-team. Still, it was fantastic that he had made the effort to send it.

I was really happy with how I played. I was riding the crest of a wave and felt confident every time I got the ball. I had a shot after five minutes that just missed the near post and smashed against the hoardings. Sheffield Wednesday's David Hirst had a go at me for not crossing it in but I know that if he'd been in the same position he'd have had a dig.

Imagine if I had scored on my England debut but never netted for Liverpool?

My job was to mark the highly-rated, Papin. He was regarded as one of Europe's best strikers and would later play for AC Milan. He kept drifting out onto the left wing and running at me but I managed to hold my own.

In the second half my confidence was sky high and when someone switched a pass out to the right wing I just killed it dead before whipping in a dangerous cross under pressure. I've seen it back on TV a few times and I'm always surprised at myself!

It was a successful night for both the team and for me personally. I got some really good press in the days that followed so I was more than satisfied.

I read an interview my granddad did in the Ellesmere Port Pioneer newspaper following the game. He said he had made every single tackle with me and was so proud that I had followed in his footsteps. He never ever took any credit for my development. He placed all the praise at Dario and his staff's feet.

It was only a few weeks after my international bow that I started to have problems with shin splints. It's an injury that stems from playing a lot of football and running on hard ground. I know a lot of tennis players get it and it's quite common.

I was informed that rest was the only cure. I remember missing training at Melwood quite a lot.

It didn't impact too much upon my displays on the pitch, however.

I finished the season in good form for Liverpool and won the FA Cup.

After I'd played in the final we joined up with England ahead of Euro 92 in Sweden. I was in the preliminary squad and was confident I would make the cut.

It transpired that Taylor had heard a rumour that I had been resting a shin injury.

I wasn't a bullshitter, so I admitted to him that I was struggling. It was still pretty sore.

I've always described it as like having glass in your shins. Not a pleasant experience I can assure you.

Whenever I put my foot down I was getting a sharp pain.

Taylor consulted his medical team and the decision was made to send me to a London hospital for further examination. I spent the day having tests and scans on my shins.

When the results came back Taylor pulled me aside.

He told me it was bad news and that I needed a lot of rest. The doctors had told him my shins were inflamed and that they weren't going to heal overnight.

He looked genuinely distraught about it. He told me I had been integral to his plans but that he couldn't chance taking me to Sweden if I was going to breakdown with injury.

I closed my eyes and let the demoralising words wash over me. I knew they would take a while to fully impact upon me.

I know some players have gone to World Cups and European Championships making out they are fit when they clearly aren't. I was always quite an honest pro and I wanted England to do well.

I understood Taylor's decision but obviously I was disappointed. To play in the Euros would have been the perfect way to top off that fairytale first season.

I'd never come up against such a combination of physical presence, skill and outright pace before but McMenemy said that he would have caused chaos for a lesser full-back. That put me back in the frame for the senior squad but I would miss the World Cup qualifiers against Poland and Norway.

Souness had been involved in discussions with Taylor over my recovery and although I felt fine heading into the summer of 1993, it was decided that it would benefit me to have a break and miss England's tour of the USA as well as the U21s' Toulon tournament.

It wasn't a very successful trip for Taylor and co. We lost to the USA and Germany but did draw with Brazil.

As a result of this hiatus, it was actually 19 months between my first and second cap.

My long-awaited second cap was against Poland in a World Cup qualifier at Wembley. It was great to be back. I had been concerned that I may turn into a one-cap wonder.

The shin splints had denied me the opportunity to establish myself for England so I was eager to show the rest of the country what I could do. I knew that once that had cleared up and I was playing well for Liverpool, then an England chance would eventually follow.

In the lead up to that match the Liverpool Echo ran a piece that promised to pay me one million Polish Zloty if I scored. I'm not certain what that converts to but they wouldn't have wanted to shell out any money, so they must have been certain that I wouldn't find the net!

We won the match 3-0 with goals from Les Ferdinand, Paul Gascoigne and Stuart Pearce.

Gazza had a great game but ended up getting booked which ruled him out of the crucial qualifier in Holland. He wasn't the only one who felt the referee's wrath either. I picked up my only ever caution for my country that night.

The match in the Netherlands was massive but proved to be a miserable occasion.

We lost 2-0 and it was highly controversial given Ronald Koeman's contribution to the evening. With the deadlock yet to be broken, he got away with a yellow card when he should have received a straight red for a professional foul on David Platt.

Platty was clean through and given his scoring record for his country you'd have fancied him to have tucked it away.

But Koeman remained on the pitch and later scored a free-kick to put Holland in control. It was a pivotal moment and ultimately ended our hopes of qualifying for USA 94.

It just added to my frustration.

I had been left out of the match after Taylor had told me he was picking Paul Parker at right back.

I wasn't impressed.

I could understand why Taylor felt Parker had more experience, but he was going to be marking Marc Overmars. The Dutch star was one of the fastest players in the game.

I had all the assets necessary to combat his threat and felt I had proved that time and time again at Liverpool against top-class opposition.

I was in Holland on that miserable night but didn't even make the bench. I had to watch my World Cup dream go up in flames from the stand. It was a helpless feeling.

I don't think Parker had a particularly bad game but there was nothing much going forward for England. I don't think Taylor wanted that. He was looking for us to keep our shape and come away with the draw. We didn't need the victory but playing for a point is always a risky strategy.

He knew I was a player that loved to get forward and obviously decided to err on the side of caution. Like I've mentioned before, I think I'm an all round right back. I have always played the position with defence as my priority. If you stick with your man and stop him you are halfway there. So if I'm asked to just sit then I feel I am more than capable of doing that.

But it wasn't to be and when we lost that match we were left needing a miracle against San Marino. We actually conceded early on which was another disaster. The lads recovered to win 7-1 but it wasn't enough and the grim confirmation came through that we had failed to qualify for the World Cup in the USA.

It was a bitter pill to swallow and another chance to play in a big international tournament had gone begging. Ironically, it would prove to be the one summer during my time with England that I was fit and raring to go. I still believed there was time for me to realise that dream of competing on the biggest stage.

Little did I know that injury would continue to be my great nemesis.

Our failure to reach the World Cup put paid to Taylor's England reign and Terry Venables was installed as a popular choice to assume control.

The former Tottenham and Barcelona boss was brought in to prepare the team for the European Championships that would take place on home turf in 1996. It was the first time England had hosted a major tournament since the 1966 World Cup and there was a feeling throughout the country that we had a squad capable of going close.

I'd be lying if I said it wasn't a major target for me at that point in my career.

Venables had two years to mould his team and I was a big part of his plans.

I started his first game in charge, a 5-0 win over Greece and was involved in other matches against Norway, Nigeria and the USA.

But it was a game versus Romania that was the beginning of the end for me. We fell behind midway through the first period to a goal from Ilie Dumitrescu, the future Tottenham midfielder. Newcastle's Rob Lee equalised just before half-time and we ended up drawing 1-1.

It was probably my worst match for England. I had a searing pain burning in my side throughout the contest and at times I was doubling over in agony. Opponents were just breezing past me.

Eventually I had to come off and Stuart Pearce replaced me as a substitute on the hour mark.

I went home and saw the doctor. The pain had started to subside so I played the full 90 minutes for Liverpool in a 3-2 loss at Blackburn.

Venables saw I had been involved and phoned me. He suggested I had made a 'miraculous recovery'.

I didn't know what to say. I couldn't explain it to him. I still didn't know what it was.

A few months later the pain returned and this time our doctor wanted to get to the bottom of it. He sent me for several tests in Liverpool. It emerged that I had a grumbling appendix and that I would need to have it removed.

It came at a bad time as England were hosting the Umbro Cup, a tournament that included Brazil, Sweden and Japan.

I phoned Venables to tell him the bad news.

He was exasperated. He paused for thought following his initial outburst of disappointment.

Terry was a great man-manager. Even though he was deeply frustrated his tone of voice shifted to one of compassion. He wished me a speedy recovery and told me to be ready for the next England get-together.

I was dismayed. I felt like I had let him down.

It also opened the door for rival right-backs to show what they could do.

Gary Neville seized the opportunity and made a solid debut against Japan. He made enough of an impression to claim the number two shirt as his own.

With Euro 96 looming ever larger on the horizon, the start of the 1995-96 season took on greater significance.

Liverpool began to illustrate just why many pundits had them down as the best football side in England, which could only have done my chances the world of good.

I was enjoying playing in such an attack-minded team but the arrival of Jason McAteer and problems in the left-back, or left-wing back area, meant Roy Evans asked me to do a job on that flank.

McAteer was an attacking midfielder by trade but produced some great performances at right wing-back and I was asked to continue on the left.

It wasn't a major problem for me. Some supporters have since said to me that it may have hampered my England hopes but I saw it differently. Venables was fully aware of what I could do at right-back. In fact, he even spoke to me about the situation when I met up with the squad over the course of the season.

I wasn't playing in any of the friendly matches but he told me not to worry. He felt that the fact I could do a job on both flanks made me more likely to be a key member of the squad in the summer. He believed it would also enhance my chances of being on the bench as I offered versatility.

I'd even switched over to the left for England during one of the friendly matches we had played so I was more than capable.

It still happens now. Glen Johnson did it for Liverpool in the second half of the 2010-11 season but I'm sure if you asked him he would always prefer his more natural position on the right.

I had come to terms with the fact Neville was the current first choice but I was more concerned with Liverpool. If I had to play on the left for the benefit of the team then that was good enough for me. I wasn't the type to start shouting about it. My club came first and if I did well for Liverpool then England recognition would follow, just like it had done in the past.

Neville gets some stick but he proved to be a consistent full-back for both club and country.

I used to travel with him from Manchester airport for England games. There were a few matches when only the two of us from the north-west area were named in the squad.

We didn't really say that much to each other. He was a lot younger than me and I suppose the Liverpool-Manchester United thing meant we weren't going to be best friends.

After my international career was over, I remember a few of the Liverpool players would return from duty moaning about his attitude towards them. Obviously he had some issues. He'd become more experienced and was perhaps too keen to express his opinion at times.

He has recently retired and suggested in his autobiography that his 10 years with England were a waste of time. I don't buy that at all. I've always found he says things to get a reaction and I think that's the case once again. Just look at him now, he was part of Roy Hodgson's back room staff at Euro 2012!

People often point to him and say there is no way he would have won 85 caps for England if I'd stayed fit. That's nice to hear and maybe that could have been the case.

If I just step back and look at what Rob Jones the right-back had in his locker then maybe you could say there was a bit more to my game. I was certainly much quicker and pace is an invaluable commodity in football nowadays.

It's easy to look back and wonder about it. I always picked up serious injuries. They were never 'niggly' ones. If I'd stayed fit and injury-free then why couldn't I have gone on to get the same amount of caps and played in World Cups?

It's frustrating when you look at it that way but I try not to dwell on it.

If I spent all of my time wondering about what might have been I'd have just ended up in a pit of depression. It was hard enough coming to terms with having to quit without wallowing in self pity.

It certainly wasn't meant to be for me at international level.

I loved playing with Macca down the right for Liverpool in the early 90s and it would have been brilliant if I'd had the chance to form a similar partnership with David Beckham for England.

I think we'd have worked well together. He's the type of professional who knows all about discipline and if I'd bombed forward I'd have had no worries that he would fill in for me. I'm sure he'd have helped to make me a better player and maybe that's why Gary won so many caps. Playing with Beckham can only have helped him improve.

It was really strange. Looking back I still cannot fathom why my body could take all the games with Liverpool and then break down ahead of England matches.

I was really looking forward to Euro 96 and was convinced I would be in the squad. But from Christmas onwards I struggled with my back, culminating in the misery of missing out on yet another tournament.

As if my back problems weren't enough an article appeared on the back pages of the newspapers soon after stating that I wouldn't be able to have sex for six months as a result!

I couldn't believe it.

I walked into Melwood one morning and the doc was laughing his head off. He pointed to the paper with far too much pleasure for my liking.

I was gobsmacked.

It was one of those interviews when you are talking about the injury and joking that it could affect your sex life. In typical tabloid style it then appears as a massive headline!

I took a bit of stick for that. I had to laugh it off but it was also a good lesson. There I was thinking I was just doing an interview about my injury heartache and all they were looking for was a sensational line.

It made me much more cautious when I did interviews after that.

I think relationships between players and reporters improved a bit as I was just finishing up. They'd go as far as to e-mail you the article with the headline before it went to print so you could raise any objections. It's a good way of doing it because players won't want to talk if they are constantly being set up.

After the Euros I never had another look in with England.

Glenn Hoddle took over and the international team moved on. I never received another call-up.

In fact, the only time I have ever spoken to him was in faith healer Eileen Drewery's house many years later. I was struggling with my knee and I ended up visiting her to see if she could do anything to help.

But it wasn't to be.

Taylor offered me the chance to stay with the squad for another week in London and watch the warm-up games.

I decided to take him up on the offer.

I was gutted to miss the Wembley friendly with Brazil. There's something special about that golden shirt and facing the samba stars wasn't an opportunity that arose very often.

The match itself became infamous for Gary Lineker's failure from the penalty spot. If he'd scored he would have equalled Bobby Charlton's record of 49 goals for England.

I watched it in the stand with Barnesy. We couldn't believe that he missed it. He was so clinical for England and it was a real shame that he didn't just hammer it hard and true. I think he's probably relived that a few times over the years and slotted it coolly into the far corner.

After that the lads all set off for Sweden. It was another low point to have to head home.

I reported to Melwood and they told me to rest up and get myself away on holiday. They didn't want to see me for six weeks.

The idea was that I would return fresh and raring to go. Unfortunately that wasn't the case. Little did I know it but this would be just the beginning of my injury nightmare.

It wasn't until the run-in to the 1992-93 season that my shin splints were finally cured. I had the operation in the October but it still didn't feel right when I returned.

It was yet more frustration and as a result I dropped down the pecking order and was involved in a few games for the U21s.

I had a blinder in a 3-0 win over Holland in the April. Lawrie McMenemy came out after the match and praised me for the way I'd handled a 6 ft 2 winger who played for PSV Eindhoven, called Peter Hoekstra.

A few of the lads had sworn by her during Hoddle's England reign and someone suggested I should give it a go.

Robbie Fowler and Macca took the piss big time but it got to the point after I was released by Liverpool, that I was willing to try anything.

It was a last resort and ultimately a fruitless one.

She was fine with me, very polite and accommodating. But it didn't really help my knee.

I saw her once a week for a few months. It was a strange experience but I suppose that illustrates just how desperate I had become to save my career.

It was during one of those weekly visits that I bumped into Hoddle.

I came down the stairs to see him standing in her kitchen with a tea bag.

He offered me a cup but I declined.

It was quite an awkward chat. We talked about the weather, the latest news headlines and even touched upon holiday plans.

He asked how my knee was coming on but there was never any mention of England.

When he had taken the job I thought I might hear from him, but I never did.

The chance was there again that day but he must've had a feeling I was finished.

When Eileen appeared they hugged and sat down to their cup of tea.

I made my excuses and sought a hasty departure.

It was all very strange and proved to be my one and only, bizarre experience of Hoddle.

CHAPTER SIX

Cows and sheep.

The doctor had said it so matter-of-factly, you'd have thought that making that particular diagnosis for a professional footballer was a day-to-day occurrence on his hospital ward.

I couldn't quite get my head around it.

Farm animals?

Yes, farm animals were behind my persistent vomiting for the previous fortnight.

I couldn't help but feel sorry for myself. It was hardly the type of routine injury to disrupt your pre-season, was it?

I lay back in my hospital bed and tried to fathom as to how I had picked up this mystery illness.

We had arrived in Norway for a training camp and I had been feeling fighting fit.

I hadn't come into contact with any cows or sheep; nor had I eaten any as part of my diet.

I was heading into my first full season as a Liverpool player and was confident I could make the 1992-93 campaign a memorable one for both club and country.

I had followed the orders of both England and Liverpool's medical staff by resting my problem with shin splints for just under two months.

I had returned to Melwood slightly earlier than scheduled and began a weight training programme that had helped me bulk up to the tune of 18 pound.

I felt fantastic and was one of the front runners in all of the initial training exercises.

But that all changed when we got to Scandinavia and I was struck down by this mystery sickness.

I was completely wiped out and couldn't stop vomiting. All of the good work I had done in the gym went to waste and I was put on a drip for several days.

It emerged that I had caught the bug through the town's drinking water. When it had rained it had filtered into the areas system from the fields where the animals were grazing.

It was a rough few weeks and set me back in my preparations.

I like to laugh about it now and say it was because I was drinking water and all of the other lads were on lager!

Think of the most awful case of food poisoning you've had and times it by five. It was that bad. I've never seen or heard of anything like it since.

It meant I didn't feature in the Charity Shield match with Leeds United.

It's always frustrating to miss out on a chance to play at Wembley but when all was said and done, I was just pleased to be on the mend.

It proved to be a disappointing afternoon for the lads.

Cantona got a hat-trick and we didn't defend particularly well.

It was a seven-goal thriller but the only part of the game I can remember was when Strachan scored the type of own goal you have nightmares about.

He got the ball stuck between his feet and ended up back heeling it over his own line. I felt for him a little bit, but not too much because Leeds ended up winning 4-3.

Souness had once again been busy in the transfer market.

He had brought in David James to rival Brucie for the goalkeeping jersey while Paul Stewart, who had always done well against us, came in from Spurs.

I was quite pleased when we signed Stewart. I remember the FA Cup final when Gazza picked up that horrific knee injury and he ran the show after Tottenham's main man had been stretchered off.

Stewart scored on his home debut in a 2-1 win over Sheffield United at Anfield, a match that also saw the opening of the Centenary stand.

But that was as good as it got for him.

I don't know if he didn't settle or what. He got on well with everyone in the changing room. He was a great lad and still turns out at charity golf events that the former players arrange from time to time.

It just didn't happen for him at Liverpool.

There was definitely a new-look to our cup-winning squad but it began to feel like a club in transition rather than one on the up.

We didn't start particularly well. We lost our first match of the season 1-0 at Nottingham Forest. It was the first ever Premier League match to be shown live on Sky Sports.

It doesn't take a genius to recognise that Sky have revolutionised the game. It's a completely different beast now and you have to hold your hand up and say the league is better for it. There's no doubt about that.

I still love going to Anfield with Declan but if I have to watch it on Sky, then they've done such a good job with their coverage over the years that I'm quite happy to sit in the armchair with a beer in hand.

You could never have envisaged it would have such an impact when we rolled up at the City Ground back in August 1992.

Souness opted to deploy three at the back as a result of an ever-growing injury list and it really backfired. Teddy Sheringham got the only goal of the game but if it hadn't been for James we would have been on the end of a real hiding.

Jamo had arrived from Watford and was widely regarded as the best young English stopper around. He was a real nutter and another prime example of the old adage that you have to be mad to be a goalkeeper.

His form was such that Souness opted to stick with him and he was a shining light in an underwhelming start to the campaign.

I had finally made my way back into the reckoning following the illness, but no sooner had I overcome that hurdle, then I was faced with another one.

My shins still weren't right. I managed to play six games before I completely broke down.

It was following a match with Chelsea that I asked for a meeting with the manager and the club's medical staff. We all agreed that I should have an operation.

My reaction was simple.

Thank god.

The final straw was after I had raced into a tackle with Dennis Wise. He caught my shin and I screamed in agony. It wasn't a nasty challenge. It was just causing me so much pain that any contact was excruciating.

I'd battled on for as long as I could but the recovery period between games was getting ridiculous.

I remember taking Paul for a birthday treat at a golf course near Tarporley. It had been a great day and a nice leisurely game but around the 16th hole I had to pack it in. I pulled my tracksuit up and showed it to him. A dark blue bubble had come up on my shin. It was like a blister but full of blood. I knew it would go down in a few days but it was obvious I couldn't carry on like that.

I think I was one of the first people ever to have an operation for shin splints. The specialists had always felt the cure for the problem was rest. But because it just wouldn't go away I eventually had to go under the knife.

It's quite a common procedure now. Former Newcastle and Manchester United striker, Andy Cole had the same operation a few years after me.

I had set the precedent and for a while medical teams across the country used to phone up our medical team at Melwood to find out how to go about it.

It wasn't a particularly nice experience.

They had to split both of my shins open. The doctor described it as a build-up of dirt that had been caused by the constant pressure of the calf grinding against it. They had to slit a big hole inside the calf to release it. Not pleasant.

I was in good company in the treatment room. Barnes, Thomas, Whelan and Wright were all out too.

It proved to be the story of our season. I think Souness only managed to get what he would regard as his strongest team out on a couple of occasions.

When I returned to action I expected to feel brand new. Sadly, that wasn't the case. The pain was still there. I began to wonder whether I would have to endure the problem for the rest of my career. At times it was quite depressing.

It was a nagging companion throughout the campaign and something I had to learn to accept.

All of the injuries meant the team had endured a mixed bag of results but there were still some positives we could point to.

It gave Souness the chance to blood some youngsters which, to be fair, he wasn't shy of doing. I was a good example of that, as was Robbie Fowler.

That year Don Hutchison and Jamie Redknapp began to feature and their performances were such that supporters were optimistic about the future, if not the present.

Souness needed more cover and bolstered his defensive ranks with the addition of Torben Piechnik.

He was a Denmark international and arrived with a fine reputation, but from day one you could see he wasn't going to be the answer to our problems.

He made his debut in a 4-2 defeat at Aston Villa, a match that was notable for several reasons.

Deano made his bow for the Midlands outfit that afternoon. I never quite understood why we sold him just prior to our trip to Villa Park. It was almost fated that he would come back to haunt us, which he did by netting a brace and causing Torben no end of trouble.

I remember one of the headlines on the back pages the next day was, 'it's no Piechnik for Torben.' It was a disappointing result and a bad start for him but you couldn't help but chuckle at the play on words.

Another moment that made that day infamous was Ronny Rosenthal's miss.

The Rocket raced in on goal, rounded the keeper and looked all set to tap home. But somehow the net didn't bulge.

Instead of coolly rolling it over the line he contrived to put his laces through it. The end result was a rising shot that crashed against the crossbar, leaving him red-faced by an incident that remains one of the most memorable blunders of recent history.

I wasn't playing that day, but as a teammate I really felt for him and it didn't help that we lost the game.

The thing that rankled most with the players was that there was no gentleman's agreement with Villa. Deano shouldn't have played. It didn't make sense to allow him to face us just 10 days after leaving. We knew what he could do and he would no doubt have been even more fired up. He will have felt he had a point to prove and maybe the shrewd thing to have done would have been to come to an arrangement to ensure he didn't play.

I suppose that's easy to say in hindsight. Liverpool didn't do it when they sold Fernando Torres to Chelsea and he made his debut against them a week later. On that occasion Kenny Dalglish masterminded a 1-0 win at Stamford Bridge and Torres was substituted, so I suppose it can go both ways.

I didn't quite understand why we sold Saunders in the first place. I thought he had done a good job for us and scored his fair share of goals.

I always find it a bit surprising that he was only at Liverpool for just over a season. It felt like longer. He was a good guy and had been really good to me when I first arrived on Merseyside.

Things may not have been going to plan but the Christmas party that year did help lift our spirits a little.

I went as the Tin man from the Wizard of Oz. We always wore some whacky costumes and I remember going as a soldier and a prisoner of war on other occasions.

We used to have a picture taken by the newspapers and we'd then get some money towards our party.

As you can imagine there are some stories that even now, we can't go into but on the whole they were just good fun. A couple of things did hit the papers from time to time and then you were in trouble at home!

If there was a picture of you being rowdy it's not as if you could claim that it wasn't you! What are you going to say? No luv, that wasn't me, there were two tin men at the party? Somehow I don't think the Mrs would buy that!

But the Christmas dos were always great. They were good for team morale and we all took the piss out of each other. It's not the same nowadays. The spotlight on players is so intense and with camera phones and things like that they can barely breathe.

There have been incidents with the likes of Manchester United and West Ham in recent years where things have been blown out of all proportion by the tabloids and I think managers prefer their players to just go out and have a quiet meal nowadays.

The New Year is a time for resolutions and an opportunity to approach things with a fresh outlook.

We tried our best to transmit that onto the pitch but the 1992-93 season continued to be highly frustrating. We seemed to move one step forward, only to take two back.

There was no solace in the FA Cup this time around either. We were drawn away to second division (League One nowadays) Bolton and found ourselves trailing in stoppage time. A huge shock was on the cards until Mark Seagraves put through his own net with virtually the last kick of the game.

We had a reprieve and welcomed them to Anfield for the replay. But we didn't learn our lesson and were deservedly beaten 2-0 on the night.

I felt Souness made a mistake in the replay. David Lee was a speedy winger and I'd played against him during my days at Crewe. He operated on the right when I was with 'the Alex' and Dario used to move me to left back to shackle him and counter his speed. The majority of the time I marked him out of the game.

He went on to have a magnificent match for Bolton on the opposite flank to me and was at the hub of all of their best moves.

We just weren't at the races and were deservedly booed off the pitch.

It meant that our season was effectively over. We had no chance of winning any silverware.

We finished sixth and were miles behind the champions Manchester United. It was a massive frustration and I felt we had seriously underachieved. It wasn't acceptable at a club like Liverpool; injuries or no injuries. We simply had to do better.

We were somewhat ashamed of some of our performances that year but ended on a high with a 6-2 home win over Tottenham. There were a lot of rumours doing the rounds that Souness had been dismissed on the morning of that game and he wasn't on the bench to watch what was arguably our best display of a very difficult campaign.

It turned out he was on a scouting trip. I think he was watching Coventry's Peter Ndlovu. The Zimbabwe international was continually linked with a move to Liverpool around that time but it never materialised.

Our failure meant there was a real determination within the ranks when we returned for pre-season training ahead of the 1993-94 season.

Souness sought reinforcements and, most notably, brought in Nigel Clough to play alongside Ian Rush a la Peter Beardsley. Cloughie had been Nottingham Forest's key man under his Dad, Brian's management and it was felt his pass and move style would make him a perfect fit at Liverpool.

Neil Ruddock was another new recruit who came into bolster the defence. He was a larger than life character and loved a practical joke or two.

He was also a tough player; a hardman who would add some extra steal to the side and give us a bit more of an aerial presence at the back.

I really believed we had made additions to the squad that would enhance our displays on the pitch.

It reflected in our results early on and we began the new term in irrepressible form.

Cloughie hit a brace to see off Sheffield Wednesday on the opening day at Anfield before a 3-1 win at QPR was followed by a 5-0 rout of Swindon Town on their own patch.

We were flying and went into the next game at home to Tottenham expecting to make it four wins out of four.

We dominated and should have won at a canter. But we got sloppy and they came away with a surprise 2-1 victory.

We still felt we had good momentum and bounced back at home to Leeds.

Rushie opened the scoring with his 200th league goal as we eased to a 2-0 win. I was heavily involved in the second. I played the ball to Molby and made an epic run from the right, all the way to the left. Molby waited and waited before picking out my dash. I found myself in a race with the onrushing goalkeeper and was brought crashing down just inside the box. The referee awarded a penalty and Jan scored to clinch the points.

Suddenly everyone was talking about Liverpool again and with four wins from our first five matches, many were tipping us for the title.

It was premature and it all went wrong soon after as September encompassed four defeats .

Souness had continued to scour the transfer market and brought in Julian Dicks at left-back.

I think the boss was looking to bring in hard men with a similar reputation to his own, but it didn't work out with Julian.

He did a great job at West Ham, but with respect, Liverpool is a different level. His knees were knackered so I have no idea how he passed his medical to make the move in the first place.

He literally had no cartilage in his knees. You knew he would always give 100 per cent and he had a great left foot on him but he lacked pace, which can be difficult for a full-back.

He bought a house up by me and we became quite friendly. Talk about two characters like chalk and cheese! But we did get on quite well off the pitch and we shared the odd pint in our local.

He made his debut in a 2-0 Merseyside derby defeat at Goodison Park. It was a desperate day for us.

Mitch Ward got their first goal when Macca only half-cleared a corner.

Macca would have been angry with himself anyway so he didn't need Brucie rushing out of goal and confronting him like he did. He totally lost his head and was completely out of order. Macca was only a young lad and it was a stupid thing to do.

I think it's something that is okay to do in the dressing room, but not on the pitch in front of goading, rival supporters.

The incident didn't do us any favours and Tony Cottee went on to seal the Blues' win.

A couple of days later Brucie and Macca had a photo taken with the Echo and were all smiles again. It was a heat of the moment thing but one that should have been avoided.

We were all a bit down after the derby and needed to pick ourselves up in time for the League Cup clash with Fulham. They were a lower division outfit back then and we were expected to boost our confidence with a comfortable victory.

Souness used the first-leg at Craven Cottage to blood a kid by the name of Robbie Fowler. He came in to partner Ian Rush and produced an accomplished debut for an 18-year-old, netting the final goal of the game in a 3-1 win.

I'd heard about this lad and been told that he had everything. Those weren't just the words of anybody, they were spoken by Steve Heighway, who had overseen Robbie's rise through the ranks.

He'd joined in training with us a few times and the thing that always stood out was the accuracy of his shooting. He was so clinical with such little back lift. It was clear he had natural ability. I'd seen it before with lads at Crewe though. They had everything to make it and then it just wouldn't happen. Thankfully that wasn't the case with Robbie.

The manager had already shown with me that he wasn't opposed to throwing youngsters in at the deep end and Robbie kept his place in the team for games against Chelsea and Arsenal. He didn't score but you could see he had bags of quality.

Fans were already beginning to tip him as Rushie's successor when Fulham came to town for the second-leg of the League Cup tie.

He became on overnight sensation, notching all five goals as we hammered the Londoners without reply. I actually had a hand in a couple of his strikes and in the days that followed I joked with him that he owed me for helping to thrust him into the national spotlight!

We became great friends during our time together at Liverpool and remain close to this day.

He was a natural goalscorer. He was similar to Rushie in the way he was always in the right place at the right time. He could just score a goal out of nowhere; a priceless commodity to have in your team.

He made a lot of goals himself but if a shot was parried or a cross was put into the six yard box, he would be there to take advantage. It was just instinctive.

Even nowadays he's still got it. We play in Masters events in Asia every year as part of the Liverpool legends team and he's as deadly as ever. He gets into situations where you think there's no chance of him scoring and then suddenly the net bulges.

Goalscoring has always been effortless for him.

The same couldn't be said of me of course.

A couple of weeks after Robbie's five-star show we played Manchester City at Maine Road and I had a great chance to open my account for the club.

Rushie put me in and I was literally on the six yard line. I *had* to score.

I fired it towards goal and it squeezed underneath the goalkeeper, Tony Coton. That took the pace off the ball slightly and as it rolled towards the line I thought I had finally done it. Suddenly Alan Kernaghan came from nowhere to hack it clear. It hit me again, rebounded towards goal but just as I was about to celebrate a bizarre effort, it hit him and trickled away to safety.

It was hugely frustrating and meant the dressing room stick continued! I did redeem myself to some extent in the final minute when I exchanged a one-two and crossed for Rushie to nod home and earn us a 1-1 draw.

After such a promising start to the campaign we were struggling to find consistency. Wins against Southampton, West Ham and Ipswich in the League Cup were followed by a demoralising 3-0 hammering away to Newcastle.

We had no fewer than 23 players on the treatment table for that encounter at St James' Park and ended up taking a serious beating. Andy Cole got a hat-trick and it could easily have been six or seven.

I was among those ruled out of action. I sustained a cartilage injury in the 2-0 win at home to West Ham and ended up needing an operation.

It meant I was set for another spell on the sidelines and also saw me miss out on England's final World Cup qualifying match with San Marino, which marked the end of Graham Taylor's reign.

We took a lot of stick for the Newcastle defeat and our hopes of winning the League Cup were ended not long after when we lost to Wimbledon on penalties in a fourth round replay at Selhurst Park.

When we beat Ipswich Town 2-1 at Portman Road on New Year's Day, a statistic that was pointed out to me summed up where we were going wrong. It was our first away win in the league since August 1993. That simply wasn't good enough for a club of Liverpool's calibre.

It was a major boost getting three points on the road but the pressure was still very much on for the visit of Manchester United three days later.

It proved to be an absolute classic. We found ourselves 3-0 down inside the first 24 minutes. I couldn't believe it. I remember Robbie blazing over a great chance inside the first minute to put us in front and after that it all went pear-shaped.

I glanced up to the Kop and saw streams of fans leaving. There was obviously a real concern that this was going to be one of the most embarrassing defeats in the history of our meetings with United.

As ever, I was marking Giggs in that game and I was disappointed that he got on the score sheet. He capitalised upon a sloppy pass by Jamie Redknapp, led Wrighty a merry dance and then clipped an unbelievable chip over Brucie.

There was nothing I could have done about it but it still smarted that my immediate opponent had inflicted a real blow.

I always loved going up against Giggs. He was the benchmark for left wingers. If you played well against him then you knew you were doing something right.

I had a competitive streak, particularly when it came to my pace. Not many players were as quick as me and if someone like Giggs knocked it into the space behind, I simply had to get there first. It was a desire that served me well as I was able to channel the right amount of aggression into the challenge too.

It was professional pride. If Giggs did get past me and clip crosses into the box then I would always reflect upon it as a bad game.

He was the player I regarded as my biggest test.

He had it all; pace, skill, vision.

We used to have some great battles but there was always a mutual respect there.

I remember when he first hit the headlines. He was wrapped in cotton wool by Alex Ferguson and wasn't really allowed to give interviews. When he did finally do one I think the press asked him five questions and one of them was whom he regarded as his toughest opponent.

He said Rob Jones.

It was great to hear and nice to know that he rated me so highly.

Whether that is still the case now is doubtful when you consider the great players he will have faced over the years in the Champions League and at international level. It would be nice to think he still put me up there though.

It's amazing to see what he has gone on to achieve in the game. He really is the perfect example of how to look after yourself and adapt your style to keep playing at the very highest level.

On that January night in 1994 he showed us just what he is capable of before Denis Irwin struck an unstoppable free-kick to put them in dreamland.

I felt we had been unlucky. Everything they had hit had gone in.

We were shell-shocked. I glanced around at some of the faces of my teammates. Most players would have looked frightened and worried about United notching up a cricket score.

But not at Liverpool.

There was an anger brewing. A sense that this was an unjust scoreline.

We just needed something to kick-start us.

Cue Nigel Clough to get the ball rolling with a superb 30 yarder at the Kop end.

The roar of the crowd was more in relief and hope rather than belief.

It was a lifeline but we still had a mountain to climb.

There was an extra zip to our play and we suddenly had a bit of momentum.

A goal prior to the interval would set us up for a huge second half and it was Cloughie who once again obliged with another clinical finish.

We were back in it. The Kop erupted and this time there was real belief in their thunderous applause.

It had been a breathtaking first 45 minutes and Cloughie had been our main man. If I'm honest, we were all a bit surprised. He'd faded away since his impressive start to life in the number seven shirt and had been moved back into central midfield following the emergence of Robbie.

It was probably his last memorable game as a Liverpool player.

It was the type of match that saw shape and tactics go out of the window.

We poured forward at every opportunity and they looked to hit us on the break.

We came close to shipping a fourth on a couple of occasions in that second half but we could also have levelled it up much earlier too. I just remember there being space everywhere.

I had to do more running than in your average game. I was bombing forward with relentless regularity and then having to race back into position. My lungs were burning but I was loving every second of it.

With time running out we gave it one last push. Stig Bjornebye picked up the ball on the left and sent in the type of delivery he had been signed for. Razor Ruddock had stayed forward from the corner and showed the desire to get there that made it one of those great headed goals. He out-jumped Bruce and thumped a stunning goal beyond Peter Schmeichel.

Bedlam.

That was the only way to describe the scenes of celebration, both on the pitch and in the stands.

We had somehow rescued a 3-3 draw in what has gone down as one of the last great games in front of the standing Kop.

I think we even had a chance to win it late on; can you imagine if we had snatched a 4-3 win against United after being 3-0 down?

Everyone remembers the 4-3 wins over Newcastle but I think that was just as good. It had extra significance to me because it was Manchester United. You don't see many teams give them a three goal head start and end up sharing the spoils.

It could have been a watershed moment for Souness but within weeks of that classic encounter he was no longer Liverpool manager.

CHAPTER SEVEN

In my first season at Liverpool the FA Cup had been a beacon of light in an otherwise very ordinary league campaign.

It had papered over cracks and convinced a few of us that we had still lived up to the club's high standards by picking up some silverware.

We'd won it the hard way with various replays en route to Wembley and there was a feeling in the dressing room that it could be a similar story in the 1993-94 campaign.

We were floundering in the Premiership and out of the League Cup so all of our eggs were in the FA Cup basket.

We had been drawn away to Bristol City in round three and felt we had enough in our locker to get through the tie.

We knew that the trip to Ashton Gate would be tricky and we'd had some poor results against lower league opponents in the preceding years. But we felt those bad experiences would aid our attempts to avoid a banana skin this time around.

The first game got underway and was quite a keenly contested match until the whole place was plunged into darkness. The floodlights had failed and despite the best efforts of Bristol City's maintenance people, it was eventually called off.

I suppose it was a headline writer's dream with what transpired in the next fortnight.

'The lights go out on the Souness era' or some garbage like that.

When the tie was eventually played we were held to a 1-1 draw. It felt more like a defeat on the journey home after it emerged that Robbie had broken his ankle. He had been such a bright spot in our season and losing him for seven weeks was going to be a huge blow.

We may have been missing our teenage hot-shot but we were still confident we would have enough in our arsenal to beat Bristol City in the replay at Anfield.

Sadly, we just didn't perform. They were the better team by a distance and deservedly pulled off a huge shock. I always remember the guy who scored the winner was called Brian Tinnion. It stands out for me as it was his goal that brought an end to the tenure of the manager who took the leap of faith and signed me for Liverpool.

I knew the knives were being sharpened when the full-time whistle blew but never envisaged that Souness would be gone within days.

It's hard to judge it like a supporter when you are a part of that changing room. It's easy for a fan to see that McMahon, Staunton, Beardsley and Houghton were being sold and replaced by inferior quality.

I have no doubt I'd have voiced my concerns if I was still stood on the Kop.

I'd worshipped them from the stands and then had the privilege to play with some of them. But as a player, you are part of a squad and your focus is always on supporting the lads that are there, not the ones who have left.

If you look at the squad Souness inherited and the one he left behind then it is obvious to everyone that the latter is far weaker in terms of overall talent and ability.

He acquired some good signings but also made some poor ones. I think he'd be the first to admit that. He's gone on record saying he wanted to change things too soon. He offloaded a few players who could still play an important role and had a lot to offer Liverpool.

I'm sure if he could have that time over again he'd do it all very differently.

A lot is made of Souness's mistakes but I think it's important to point to some positives too.

He did a great job in helping to bring through some of the younger lads and if you speak to Robbie, Macca, Redders and myself, we only have good things to say about him.

It's the more senior players at the time that have an axe to grind. I know Ronnie Whelan had a fair bit to say about Souness in his autobiography and most of it was negative.

The older lads thought he could have used their experience a lot more. They felt he showed them a lack of respect, particularly when he appointed Wrighty as captain not long after he arrived from Derby County.

He didn't listen to the advice of the likes of Barnesy and Rushie. That was a big mistake.

He should have got them all on his side but he went about it differently. He came in and stamped his foot down. If I'm completely honest, I don't think he had the full support of the dressing room at any point during his spell in charge.

There was a definite split. Souness was sticking to his guns and some of the changes he made didn't go down well.

I think the interview he did with *the Sun* on the anniversary of the Hillsborough disaster was the beginning of his downfall. We went on to win the FA Cup that year but his article with *that* newspaper meant he didn't have the backing of the fans.

That's virtually unheard of when it comes to Liverpool. I think it's only Roy Hodgson who hasn't had the support of the Anfield faithful in my time following the Reds. Plenty of managers have had their tough spells but one thing they have generally been able to rely on is the club's fan base.

Souness lost that when he gave the interview to *the Sun* in the aftermath of his heart surgery.

I don't know why he did it. It was a really strange move and I know there are a lot of fans that still haven't forgiven him.

It was a huge error of judgment and I'm sure he's looked back and thought 'what the fuck did I do that for?'

There were more than a few players in his squad who had been at Hillsborough and I know it upset them.

It irritated me too.

I was young and still a relative newcomer to the side so I just kept my head down and didn't talk about it. But one of my mates had died at Hillsborough.

His name was Christopher Devonside and he had played in the same football team as me at Meadow Junior School. He was a great lad who lost his life as a result of a terrible injustice.

I still see his Dad, Barry every now and then. You only have to look into his eyes to see what that tragic afternoon has done to him and his family.

It is a very raw topic, even now, over two decades on.

So, for Souness to give that interview and allow it to be published on the third anniversary of the disaster quite rightly led to condemnation and anger.

I saw him speak about it on *Goals on Sunday* on Sky Sports not so long ago when he once again stressed the error of his ways. It's clearly haunted him and it is a very sad situation.

He had agreed to be interviewed and photographed in his hospital bed while he watched our FA Cup semi-final replay win over Portsmouth. He insists to this day that he was unaware it would be published on the anniversary and was horrified to see the image used was one of him smiling and kissing his partner.

I understand his sentiments about the suitability of the photograph but personally believe he should never have granted that particular newspaper any access.

He gave a big apology in the Manchester United programme in our final home game of the 1991-92 season. It was something he would have wanted to do regardless of any advice from the club in terms of damage limitation. He stressed that the majority of the money he was paid was going to charity.

You could see he was distraught about what had happened and wanted to repair any damage.

But it was done.

Once you do something like that, then as soon as results aren't going as you would hope, you are in trouble. Okay we went on to win the FA Cup but looking back, I think it was always a matter of time until he left.

Aside from that huge error of judgment, for me, Souness will always be a great manager.

At the end of it all he was the one who took a chance on me and gambled in a massive game that ultimately gave me the opportunity to play football at the highest level. I will always appreciate that.

I met him on the beach in Dubai in the summer of 2011. It was the first time I had seen him since he left Liverpool. It was quite amazing that our paths had never crossed properly in the time that followed, but it was fantastic to meet him and have a chat.

He told me that he regretted what had happened with *the Sun* article and the way he had treated some of the older players. He knows he made huge mistakes.

When he left that was it. He didn't come into the dressing room to say goodbye. I'd like to have said my own personal farewell to him, simply to thank him for making all my dreams come true.

But he was gone and Liverpool moved on.

There were suggestions that the board had decided to get rid of him because they wanted someone who would be a bit more lenient towards the players. There was a feeling that Souness had been too hard on us and that the way forward would be for someone with a more mild temperament to take control.

I can only really speak from my own experiences and have to say that I always found him very accommodating. He'd bought me and I'd done well for him, so I suppose there would be no reason for him to come down on me about anything.

Some of the lads that he bought, who perhaps didn't do the business, felt that he was a bit cold with them. I would hear snippets from different players and they would say that when you were out injured he would rarely talk to you.

I think that was just the passion and desire to win that is instilled in him. He wanted every player fit and ready to help Liverpool fight for honours. It hurt him if any member of his squad didn't have the same burning will to win.

We were talking about him at one of our get-togethers with the legends last year and Roy Evans just told us to forget about all of that. For him, the main thing was that Souness was a sensational player. It's something that gets missed now. People dwell on his managerial record when they should remember just how good he was. He must definitely go down as one of the top 10 players in Liverpool's history.

It was typical Roy, always seeing the best in someone. I had always had a massive respect for him.

Once Souness had gone, there was only one man who the players wanted to take charge.

Alongside Ronnie Moran, he had experienced the great highs as well as some lows for Liverpool over the years.

He'd won countless titles with the reserves and knew how to handle the players. He'd learned from the likes of Shankly, Paisley and Joe Fagan, so in our eyes there was no-one better to take charge.

Liverpool's tradition was always to promote from within and it was obvious he wouldn't come in and disrupt the camp in the same way Souness's arrival from Rangers obviously did.

Let's be clear though. It was a very difficult job.

We were out of all of the cups and were miles off the pace in the league. It was obvious to everyone that the remainder of the season would be about Roy assessing the squad and planning for a summer of activity in the transfer market.

As a result, it was a largely forgettable run-in.

We beat Everton 2-1 in a Merseyside derby at Anfield that saw the Toffees strike first. The match was live on Sky and I later found out that they missed Rushie's equaliser because of all of the replays they were showing of Dave Watson's opener!

Robbie returned in that game and scored a fantastic winner at the Kop end just before half-time. Not a bad way to sign off the final derby in front of one of the world's most famous standing areas.

I was marking Peter Beagrie on that occasion. Games against him always stood out because he was so tricky. It almost made me laugh once I got to know him because he would never cross it when he first shaped to deliver. He would always cut back inside, twisting and turning. I got to the point where I never put my foot out to block the cross and I always seemed to nullify his threat. But he was a very talented player.

Our last home match of the season before the Kop underwent an all-seater face-lift saw us welcome Norwich to Anfield.

There was a real interest from the media in the lead up to what was effectively a nothing game in terms of the league table. The Canaries had enjoyed a sensational season, particularly given their foray into Europe where they had beaten the mighty Bayern Munich on their own turf.

Jeremy Goss had scored a stunner in that game and he did it again with a goal that was fitting to say goodbye to the Kop. It was just a shame it didn't come from the boot of a Liverpool player.

Prior to kick off the club had made a big deal of the occasion with the likes of Billy Liddell, Dalglish, Albert Stubbins and Joe Fagan in attendance. Fagan was accompanied by Jessie Paisley and Nessie Shankly while Craig Johnston had flown in all the way from Australia to say his own goodbye.

It made it even more disappointing that we didn't put in one last home performance to sign off a very forgettable campaign. We finished eighth.

As I left the turf I turned and had one last, lingering look at the Kop in all its glory. Just a few years earlier I had stood there as a fan. It reminded me of how lucky I was to be playing for the club I loved. It made me even more determined to secure success in the future.

It was clear that changes were needed first of all and Roy set about making some significant ones.

Out went the likes of Dicks, Piechnik and Hutchison. Don paid the price for his off-the-field antics and his departure perhaps illustrates that Roy was ready to make an example of anyone who crossed the line.

He would deal with them in a firm way, if necessary, which is contrary to what the media would have you believe in the years that ensued.

There was also a fond farewell to some illustrious figures. Ronnie Whelan and Bruce Grobbelaar both saw their Anfield careers come to a close while Steve Nicol also moved on to pastures new later in the season.

August finally arrived and we began with real intent. A 6-1 mauling of Crystal Palace at Selhurst Park was followed by a 3-0 rout of Arsenal at Anfield. Robbie further enhanced his reputation with a four and a half minute first-half hat-trick that has gone down in Liverpool folklore.

It began an incredible run for him against the Gunners. I know from talking to them on England duty, that a few of their players were sick of the sight of him as the years went by! It was all the more impressive when you consider that back four was regarded as the meanest defence around.

That was one of the key areas Roy wanted to improve at Liverpool. He recognised he had a wealth of attacking talent at his disposal and that wins would be easier to come by if we were more solid.

The board backed him with some considerable funds and Coventry's Phil Babb, who had starred for the Republic of Ireland in the summer's World Cup finals, joined for a British record transfer fee for a defender.

He was followed by highly-rated Wimbledon centre back John Scales.

All of a sudden we had some great option at the heart of our defence and we were looking like a club on the up once again.

The arrival of that particular duo resulted in a change in system and a shift in style for myself.

We were now playing a 3-5-2 formation in which I was operating as a right-wing back instead of in a more orthodox role. It gave me more attacking licence but also meant a hell of a lot more running.

I had played the same position at Crewe on various occasions so I was relatively comfortable with it.

The system was something we knew we had to work on both on the training pitch and in matches if we were to make a success of it.

Gradually we came to terms with what we needed to do. Macca was one of the main beneficiaries of the switch.

He revelled in a free role just behind the two strikers and became our most influential player. Teams realised that you had to stop Macca if you were going to halt Liverpool and he had to get used to a fair few opponents opting to man to man mark him.

Looking back I feel we needed to be more flexible. It was fine when the 3-5-2 was working and we were beating teams, but on days when we weren't playing well or the opponent was coping with what we threw at them, maybe we needed to be able to adapt to a different system to find a way of winning the match.

Of course, it wasn't just us. Most teams back then stuck to what they knew. Nowadays I think the best sides have a lot more fluidity to their play. Forwards can swap roles and occupy different positions throughout a game. This leaves opposition defences always having to re-adjust.

I think the top managers are able to see when things aren't working with a particular system and are bold enough to make the change midway through a match.

We didn't have that adaptability but you could see as the season progressed that we were a real work in progress.

We were doing well in the Coca-Cola Cup and when Rushie bagged a hat-trick in a tough fourth Round clash at Blackburn we started to believe we could win it.

The quarter-final draw pitted us against Arsenal and again Rushie was the match winner when he finished a free-kick that was right off the training ground. It's always a great buzz when that type of idea comes off in a match and that one worked a treat.

It set up a two-legged semi-final against Crystal Palace. We were massive favourites but needed an injury-time winner from Robbie to give us a narrow 1-0 advantage at Anfield.

At this point we were in the top four in the league and also doing well in the FA Cup. We felt we were finally back where Liverpool belonged, in the mix for the top honours.

We managed to see off Palace in the second-leg courtesy of that man Robbie again, meaning we were off to Wembley once again.

We were riding the crest of a wave heading into an FA Cup quarter-final at home to Tottenham. We really fancied ourselves and looked on course for the last four when you know who struck in the first half.

But Spurs rallied to level and then stunned us in the dying moments when Jurgen Klinsmann fired a winner at the Kop end.

It was a real kick in the teeth and probably the low point of an otherwise great season. We felt we weren't clinical enough that afternoon and paid the price for missed opportunities. We were sure we hadn't been outplayed.

A satisfying 2-0 win over United was then sandwiched between a shock Anfield loss to Coventry and a goalless draw at Spurs ahead of Roy's first showpiece final as Liverpool manager.

Bolton Wanderers were the opposition and it was an occasion that proved Macca really had arrived as a world class performer.

We all knew how good he was but that day at Wembley was Macca at his best.

We controlled most of the game and Bolton only threatened sporadically. Macca was the difference.

He opened the scoring not long before half-time when he drifted in that elegant way of his, beyond Alan Stubbs, past another defender before passing the ball into the far corner.

If that was an impressive goal, then his second was right out of the top drawer.

Again he cut in from a wide position, skinned three Bolton players - including Jason McAteer who he would remind on many occasions in the years ahead – and curled another lovely finish in at the far post.

Alan Thompson did pull a goal back for Bolton late on with a real belter but we held firm to clinch a richly-deserved triumph.

I know the League Cup is seen as a trophy that isn't as important as others but for us, particularly at that time, it emerged as a priority. We were in our first full season under our new manager and had a young squad that people were tipping as future title winners. We knew it would be a psychological bonus to pick up our first piece of silverware under Roy and it was a great feeling to come out on top. It had been three years since the FA Cup win over Sunderland and that was regarded as a real drought for Liverpool.

I know Roy was made up to be amongst the honours for the first time as the gaffer. I really liked him as a boss. He is a real gentleman of the game.

I was also chuffed for Rushie. He'd been there and done it all with Liverpool but to lift the cup as the captain was a special achievement for him and one that I know he regards as a high point in his time with the club.

It would be fair to say that our season petered out after that. We did our best to try and kick on but as is often the way with a side that has won a trophy, there was a drop in concentration.

It wasn't a conscious shift in our focus. It's strange how often it happens. We just didn't have the consistency to push on. It was something observers suggested would come as we matured as a team.

I couldn't offer any explanation for our dip, particularly as I had to watch us go through the motions from the sofa.

I was ruled out of action from April onwards with tooth trouble after having an operation to have three wisdom teeth removed. My face had swollen up so much you actually wouldn't have recognised me.

It capped a nightmare nine months in which I had three spells in hospital.

It's probably the most painful thing I've suffered with. My mouth was swollen for two weeks and I looked like the elephant man. I knew some fans were wondering why I wasn't training, after all, I'd only had my wisdom teeth out. It sounds stupid, but out of all of the injuries and problems I've had over the years, that caused me the most pain. It was agony.

I woke up from the initial operation and had all yellow across my chest. I asked the doc what it was and he told me that it was bruising from where the dentist had been kneeling on my chest to pull out the teeth!

It sounded a bit unorthodox, particularly on a professional footballer! Maybe he was a Man U fan or an Evertonian!

The infection left me feeling very sorry for myself and I needed all of my will power just to potter about the house.

Not that my interest in what my teammates were up to waned in any way. The final match of the season would prove to have huge implications for the Premiership title race. We faced Kenny Dalglish's Blackburn at Anfield with Manchester United having to win at West Ham and hope Rovers didn't to clinch the championship.

The mind games were in overdrive in the week leading up to the game. Alex Ferguson was suggesting we wouldn't want United to be crowned champions and would just roll over and allow Blackburn to win.

A lot of the lads were fairly pissed off about that and rightly so. I think even the majority of supporters would take offence. Sure, they'd love United to miss out on honours but when the game gets underway, most fans can't help but want their team to do the business.

As it happened we all got what we wanted - United aside.

We came from behind to win 2-1 in injury-time when Redders scored that famous free-kick that left Kenny aghast. Thankfully, West Ham had done their part at Upton Park and held United to a draw, which meant Blackburn were champions.

It was a great day. I watched the game from the directors' box and was made up for Kenny. All of the fans stayed behind to rejoice in Blackburn's success, but there was an underlying feeling of envy there.

We wanted to achieve the success they were savouring and we felt we were on our way towards doing that.

CHAPTER EIGHT

You've all heard the stories.

Crazy, drunken nights on the town, celebrity parties and the more ludicrous suggestion of rampant sex orgies.

These were the alleged off-the-field activities that prevented Liverpool from winning the Premiership title.

Most was tabloid hyperbole, but mud as they say, tends to stick.

I can't quite put my finger on when the infamous Spice Boys tag first raised its ugly head, but the two words still make me wince to this day.

It may well have been prior to the run-in to the 1995-96 season but when I think back that is the time period that stands out.

It was blown out of all proportion.

We'd emerged as a team that many pundits were now recognising as a serious threat to Manchester United but our inconsistency led to murmurs that we didn't take our football seriously.

I don't know if it was envy, sheer malice or an agenda to sell more newspapers but anything our lads took an interest in away from the pitch received a negative write-up.

We had McAteer doing a shampoo advert, David James modelling for Armani, players being snapped at big celebrity parties and Redders going out with the pop star, Louise.

These were seen as distractions that were costing us victories on the pitch.

The fact that the game's other top names were enjoying a similar lifestyle in their spare time seemed to conveniently go unnoticed.

I remember Barnesy suggesting that the boss should have put a stop to all of it right away.

He reckoned it was just giving the media ammunition to twist the off-the-field dalliances into the explanation for our inconsistency on the pitch. He was right of course, but you can't keep players on a leash 24/7.

Roy started to get a lot of stick for being too lenient but I can assure you he wasn't.

He's a nice guy but he knew when he needed to shout or get his point across. He'd have a pint with us every now and then but a lot of managers did that in those days. It's changed a lot but in my opinion he didn't do anything to cause us to question his authority.

You've all probably heard the stories about pranks some players allegedly played upon him.

The likes of Stan Collymore and Razor Ruddock will tell tales about how Roy didn't command respect and was too easy on the players, but what can you do with characters like them? We all know what type of lads they are and they attracted that kind of attention wherever they played – not just at Liverpool.

I was never witness to anything that undermined Roy and to be honest, it doesn't fit with the man I dealt with in the dressing room. He was a good guy but he was strong.

He came down really hard on the likes of Ruddock and Molby over their respective weight problems. You have to remember that it is never as simple as treating everyone the same. A good manager knows that he has to be hard on some players and more encouraging with others. You need to work out how to get the best out of specific members of your squad. I thought Roy was great at that sort of thing, despite what Stan and others might say.

Stan was a big, powerful forward with pace, skill and a superb eye for goal. He had the lot and I was buzzing when we signed him from Nottingham Forest. He quickly forged a deadly partnership with Robbie and appeared destined for greatness.

But something was never right upstairs and I think the issues that plagued him throughout his career proved that it didn't matter who his manager was; he was always a disruptive influence.

He wouldn't make the move to live in Liverpool and was determined to drive up from Cannock every day. He would miss training a lot and even Ronnie Moran, who is as strict as they come, gave up on him. I lost count of the number of times the management gave him the hair-dryer treatment, but it was in one ear and out the other.

It didn't bother him but it showed a real lack of respect. If Ronnie or Roy shouted at me, I'd be instantly apologetic.

Overall, I think Roy did okay as Liverpool manager. Maybe that isn't what is expected; Liverpool should be winning titles year in, year out. But that's not really happened for 20-plus years now.

Roy got us to within striking distance of top spot on two or three occasions and with a bit more luck we may well have won one. If we'd managed to do that, I think we would have gone on to clinch a couple more. We certainly had the talent at our disposal and not many people would argue against the suggestion that we played the best football in the country when we were on song. Our problem was that we didn't grind out enough results when we had an off day.

Man United were always just that little bit more consistent.

It was such a sad situation because in the summer of 1995 it was all looking so positive.

I was enjoying playing at wing back and didn't see the signing of Jason McAteer as an immediate threat to my place.

It was only when I was ruled out with another injury that Roy was forced to try Jason in my position in the 2-2 draw with Manchester United at Old Trafford. It was the match that saw Robbie upstage Cantona's comeback from his infamous kung-fu attack on a fan.

I thought Jason did really well but it didn't mean I made an immediate switch to the left side as some people now assume.

It was an injury to Phil Babb in December that saw Roy move Steve Harkness to the left-side of the three centre backs. Jason played right wing back and I slotted in at left wing back.

We hammered United 2-0 at Anfield during that time, and I mean hammered. Robbie hit another double but we could have smashed five past them quite easily if it hadn't been for Schmeichel.

We'd had such a bad run from Halloween through to the start of December that I think our upturn in fortunes meant Roy was happy to stick with a winning side. We'd gone out of the UEFA Cup to Brondby, been beaten in the League Cup by Newcastle and lost three out of four league games. Had it not been for such a poor run then maybe we could have won the title that year. It's easy to say in hindsight but it certainly left us with it all to do.

A 20-match unbeaten run in all competitions followed as we showed just why we were being touted as the best football-playing side in the country. I think that sequence of results coupled with the fact we didn't have a top left-back at the time, saw me become our regular left-wing back.

We had Harkness and Stig Inge Bjornebye, who had faded off the scene at that point, so it became a case of it being me or nobody, especially when Harks moved to centre back.

I never envisaged that Jason would go on to take my place on a permanent basis. He was an attacking midfielder who had scored plenty of goals for Bolton Wanderers. That was where he made his name.

But he sparkled in the new role and was a revelation going forward. He wasn't as strong defensively but he was devastating in attack.

We were a side that always dominated possession, no matter who we played against, so perhaps it wasn't so important that he was solid. It just meant that the right-sided central defender would have to make sure he covered the gaps being left by Jason bombing forward.

The difference between our two styles was simple. I defended first and then looked to get forward when the time was right. That is essentially what a right-back is all about. My aim is always to prevent a winger going beyond me.

Jason was more attack-minded and would prioritise getting forward.

We had become rivals for the right-wing back berth but we were great friends off the pitch. He had slotted straight into the piss-taking culture at Melwood and had earned himself the nickname 'Dave' from *Only Fools and Horses.*

The lads said he was so dopey that he should be called Trigger, but because I had the unenviable honour of that, they called him Dave. It was the name by which Trigger referred to Rodney and it stuck with Jason from the word go.

It's funny because fans still remember that rivalry like it was yesterday and it's great to hear their views on the team when we meet up with them on various trips with the legends.

They know more about me than I do! They tell me when I played this game or did a piece of skill in a certain match. It's great to reminisce with them and quite often they help me to remember a moment in my career that I had previously forgotten.

We were in Ireland having a drink following a game last year and Gary Gillespie was talking about the 1988 team, a side regarded as one of the best Liverpool line-ups of all-time.

He said that the only person sat at the table that would have got in that starting XI was me. He shocked me with that statement to be honest.

It caused quite a stir and a few of the other lads, great Liverpool players in their own right, asked why they wouldn't have got in.

Gary explained that he just felt that I would have fitted into their style of play perfectly.

I don't think it went down too well with Jason! He makes me laugh because he is so competitive over our impact during that era. He gets all defensive about who was the best right back.

We'll be signing autographs at an ex-player event and some fans will come up to me and tell me I'm the best right-back the club has ever had. When I turn to talk to him he has got a right face on him. I always laugh and ask him why he's so upset, after all, he wasn't a right back. He was a midfielder or an attacking wing-back.

In the 1995-96 season he really was a major factor in our superb form leading into March.

One game that stands out for me during that time was when we defeated Leeds 5-0 at Anfield. We were leading 1-0 when I got in on the left flank and was clean through on goal. I thought the moment had finally come when Gary Kelly came from nowhere and hauled me down.

The referee pointed to the spot and shaped to give Kelly the red card. I remember trying to talk the official out of it but he stood by the letter of the law and gave him his marching orders.

Kelly was a good lad so I felt a bit sorry for him, although he had cost me my moment of glory! I was in a great position, bearing down on goal on my right foot. Who knows, maybe it is a blessing that he brought me down given my record.

I never liked seeing anyone sent for an early bath. I suffered the indignity just twice in my Liverpool career. The first was at the start of the 1993-94 season. We were playing away to Coventry City and I was shown two yellow cards within seconds of each other. They were niggly fouls more than anything.

Souness wasn't happy with it because he felt the referee, Keith Burge, had been conned by Roy Wegerle. I missed the derby because of that so I was a bit pissed off with Wegerle too. I was asked about his role in the incident after the match but refused to comment. He certainly made the most of it.

Nowadays you get a yellow card for almost any type of foul. Back then it wasn't quite as strict but I think it was a result of one of those pre-season meetings referees have to decide what to clamp down on.

I don't think I deserved to be sent off and Souness let fly in the papers. The fact we lost the match 1-0 didn't help matters. Incidentally, Phil Babb, a future teammate was the unlikely goalscorer.

The other time I saw red was in a League Cup tie up at Sunderland in October 1995. I was guilty of a late tackle on Michael Gray and it seemed to wind up his teammates. Martin Smith responded by flying in on Barnesy and I just lost it. I think it was a bit of handbags at dawn but the referee had no option. We were both given our marching orders. Thankfully we went on to win 1-0 thanks to a goal from Robbie. I apologised after the game. I wasn't exactly known for that kind of reaction and I resolved to never do it again.

So I knew exactly how Kelly felt.

I don't think it had any bearing on what was a very one-sided contest. The win over Leeds illustrated that we were in top form and edging our way into striking distance for the title when we were surprisingly beaten 1-0 at Nottingham Forest.

It set us up for two massive matches against Aston Villa, who were also in the mix at the top of the table and expected to provide a real test of our credentials.

It didn't turn out that way. We blew them away with one of the best first half performances I have ever been involved in.

Robbie was unplayable in that first 45 minutes. He scored an incredible goal at the Kop end when he did Steve Staunton with a sublime flick before crashing a thumping drive into the far corner from 25 yards.

He would come back to haunt Villa again a few weeks later when we beat them 3-0 in the FA Cup semi-final at Old Trafford.

He was named Young Player of the Year for the second consecutive season around that time and I felt he was a tad unlucky not to earn the senior gong as well.

I always thought he deserved more of a chance with England. Yes, Alan Shearer was a sensational number nine, but I'd have liked to have seen Robbie alongside him. I guess he was just unlucky that Teddy

Sheringham formed such an impressive link up with Alan. Still, I'd have given him more of a shot at that time because he was arguably the most in-form youngster on the planet.

Our FA Cup semi-final success set us up for a league showdown with Kevin Keegan's Newcastle. We still had an outside chance of winning the title and the Magpies were floundering having flittered away what had seemed like an unassailable 12 point lead.

We got off to a brilliant start when Stan crossed for Robbie to head the opener inside the first minute.

We knew they could be got at defensively but we were also well aware of the arsenal of attacking talent they had.

Again, this was a game where I felt the manager should have shifted me to the flank where the most danger was likely to come from. David Ginola had been sensational for the Magpies and I was sure I would have been better equipped to deal with him.

We eventually let them back into it through Les Ferdinand and then Ginola raced through to make it 2-1 at the interval. To be fair to Jason, I don't necessarily think that the second goal was his fault. They caught us out on the break and he was left too far up-field. When you play the three centre backs you need the right-sided one to move across and cover the winger but we were too stretched.

It had been an entertaining first period under the Anfield floodlights but the 40,702 packed inside the ground that night were about to be treated to an exhibition of football that is still recalled with vivid detail to this day.

We kicked off attacking the Kop end and immediately threw caution to the wind. It was a case of you attack, we attack. It was truly lung-bursting stuff, particularly if you were playing wing-back.

We managed to pull level when Robbie finished off a mazy run from Macca with a cracking shot from the edge of the box.

The atmosphere really was electric. I think that was rubbing off on all of the players because defensive shape had gone out of the window. We were pushing forward so much that we left huge gaps at the back. Tino Asprilla made us pay when he poked home their third of the night.

Against any other team it would have been curtains, but Newcastle's defence always gave you some hope and with our attacking players you knew we'd carve out a chance or two before the night was out.

Our third of the game came courtesy of Stan but he owed it all to Jason. He'd had a stormer surging down the right and it was his teasing centre that allowed Stan to ghost in and level it up at 3-3.

A draw wasn't good enough for us if we had any hopes of winning the title and we kept pouring forward. I think Keegan may look back now and wish he'd shut up shop and seen it out for the point. But it wasn't their way and we made them pay.

Barnes and Rushie rolled back the years with a series of one-twos as we entered stoppage-time. Barnesy showed all of the composure and vision that had made him such a class act for so long when he picked out Stan on the far left of the penalty area. He took a touch and crashed home the winner at the near post. Cue delirium and the etchings of another classic encounter in the Anfield annals.

Everyone was buzzing in the dressing room but we were all completely shattered too.

 I always remember a quote from the boss following that game. He told the newspapers that he had met a young boy afterwards who had been attending his first ever match at Anfield. He had said he felt sorry for him because he would expect every game to be like that and could end up disappointed. I knew exactly where he was coming from. It was a privilege to play in such an incredible encounter and remains one of the best games I ever played in for Liverpool.

Once again the title talk gathered momentum but it only lasted a matter of days. We travelled to Coventry the following weekend and ended up losing 1-0. We carved out a whole host of chances but just couldn't convert. It proved to be a truly depressing afternoon. Not only did we see our championship hopes evaporate but we also lost Harks to a horrific double leg break.

Our league season dropped away after that. It was disappointing, especially as it came so soon after the euphoria of Newcastle.

It was Rushie's last season with us. He had played second fiddle to Robbie and Stan for much of the campaign and you could tell he believed he was leaving the club in good hands. He revealed he was on his way to Leeds, bringing an end to a glorious second spell in red. We gave him a guard of honour in our final home match against Middlesbrough and he scored on his last league appearance at Manchester City.

But we all knew how he really wanted to sign off; clutching an FA Cup winners' medal at the expense of Manchester United.

They had just secured another league title and were eager to do the 'double'. It was the final everyone wanted to see and we were quietly confident we could turn them over having been the better team in both league encounters.

The club had mourned the loss of Bob Paisley back in February and the older generation of supporters felt it would be fitting to dedicate an FA Cup triumph to his memory.

Suddenly there was a lot of pressure being heaped upon us. From being a team edging closer towards success, we were now expected to go out and deliver.

If that wasn't enough of a burden to carry, we set ourselves up for an almighty fall with those infamous white suits.

It has to be up there as the worst thing I've ever worn. They were an absolute joke.

Jamo's contract with Armani meant he was privy to some really nice gear. He suggested he could get us some top of the range cup final suits, so we left him to it.

I think we all regretted that within minutes of turning up for the fitting. Quite a few of the lads weren't best pleased. It might well have looked good on Jamo but it certainly didn't work for all of us!

I think if we'd won 5-0 it would have been seen as some crazy way of inspiring us and making us relax. As it happened it just added further pressure to the occasion. Maybe Roy should have taken a look at the suits and said 'there's no way you are wearing them.'

But it's easy to point fingers now.

The spotlight was firmly upon us and United were calm and composed having just clinched the title. What I found a bit unfair was that United had some players who were doing similar to what our lads were.

You had the likes of Lee Sharpe, Beckham and Giggs. They were all pin ups linked to different celebrities. The difference was that they were winning trophies.

When I meet up with some of the older generation of ex-Liverpool players for legends matches, they tell some extraordinary stories. They got up to allsorts back then but the media coverage was not as intense at that time. They were also part of a winning team that clocked up two or three medals per season.

We were always on the cusp of winning something. We never truly realised the potential we had. I think we had the most frightening attacking players in the country and we certainly played the best football on our day. We just didn't produce when it mattered most.

The final itself turned out to be an awful game.

We didn't recreate the type of performance that had seen us outshine United home and away earlier in the season. It was a very cagey match and it had extra-time written all over it.

Redders had a great chance to give us the lead just before half-time while Jamo made a cracking save to deny Cantona in the second half.

One goal was always going to win it and unfortunately for us they got it through Cantona's volley. I was actually on the line and didn't react in time. When I see the slow motion replay now I always expect myself to

Celebrating our 10th wedding anniversary

Sue and I with Macca and Victoria on one of our many nights in Madrid

I always felt great pride representing my country

In the dressing room after a game

Trying to keep spirits up with my daughter Amy after finding out I'll never play football again!

Sue and I at a charity event

Another night out with my soulmate

The Jones' and the Thomas' relaxing in Majorca

At last! A goal for Liverpool in the Masters!

The opening of our first nursery in Abu Dhabi

Family time! Sue, Natalie, Amy, Declan and I make a new friend

Celebrating in Jersey

Four generations of the Jones'

Always love going back to Anfield

chest it away or get my leg high enough to deflect it to safety. But it's in the net before I react and you can see the dismay on my face.

I've had fans ask me why I moved out of the way and I always explain that I was trying to lift my knee to block it but couldn't react fast enough. There's no way I'd have ever tried to get out of the way of a shot and the suggestion is quite frankly, disrespectful to a professional footballer.

The only other option would have been to handle it, get sent off and hope Jamo saved the spot kick. It's easy to analyse it now. It all happened in a split second and sadly, I couldn't prevent it from hitting the back of our net.

Jamo even tried to blame me following the game because he didn't want people questioning his poor punch from the corner. He would often try to do that and we quickly got wise to his inability to take criticism for errors. The way I always looked at it was that if you made a mistake you held your hand up and got on with it.

It always amazes me how football is decided by such minor details. If I had somehow deflected that on to the crossbar and we had gone on to win it in extra-time, it would have gone down as a great moment in my career. On the other hand it proved to be a real low point.

It ensured that I would endure a night of both physical and emotional pain.

I'd been playing in agony for as long as I could remember. It must have been as long as 12 months since I had been playing completely pain free. I was really suffering with my back.

I spent a lot of time with the physios getting massages but the problem persisted. Eventually I was sent away for a scan. It came back completely clear. There were no hot spots or anything.

The medical staff were happy with what they had received and continued to treat it as a muscular problem.

I was constantly moaning about it. I was really struggling but they kept pointing to the scan results. I went along with it and then had a cortisone injection to try and settle any inflammation. That didn't work so I just soldiered on.

I wasn't really missing any training or games with it. But when I came off the pitch at Wembley that afternoon I turned to the club doctor and said, 'look we are going to have to sort this out.'

At this point I was having real trouble turning and reacting to things during matches. I insisted that I should see another specialist.

By coincidence, one of the practices I attended was back in Crewe. I went along and spent the day with the specialist. It involved a variety of scans and treatments. Eventually I had the answer.

It wasn't good news.

He came through the door and put all the paperwork on the table.

- Right. I've found the problem. Were you hoping to be in the squad for Euro 96?

- Well, yes of course.

In a strange way I was relieved when he told me he had an answer. But that question about the Euros threw me off guard. I'd been in the squads leading up to the finals and felt I would be involved. The next thing he said quite literally knocked me for six.

- Well, you can rule that out.

It was then that he pulled out an X-ray that showed the right vertebrae was cracked. He told me that I would need three or four months of complete rest. That meant no gym work, no cycling - nothing.

I returned to Melwood to show our medical team. Everyone was stunned. No-one could quite understand how both the initial X-ray and scan hadn't picked it up.

The problem was tucked around a corner but this scan had probed all around my body and picked it up from a different angle.

Like I say, I was glad in some ways because not knowing was the worst part of it all.

However, it also meant I was going to miss out on another major tournament with England.

To cap off my misery it was a competition taking place on home soil and we went on to reach the semi-finals. We should probably have won the trophy but once again Germany proved unbeatable in the penalty shoot-out.

The doctors at Melwood reiterated their instructions. I wouldn't be able to do anything. I just needed to rest up. No weights, no light jogging, just rest for four months.

I didn't know what to do with myself. I went over to Malaysia and opened a bar and I started hanging out with Noel and Liam Gallagher from Oasis.

I'd got tickets for Noel and his future wife, Meg Matthews to go and watch the FA Cup final against Man United. They were sitting next to my Dad, which was a bit of an experience for him!

We ended up in some bar that night and there's a picture of me sitting next to him absolutely bollocksed with a bottle of Jack Daniels on the table.

I had to vent the frustration of losing that game somehow and when you consider the white suits and the late heartache of Cantona's goals, JD seemed a good option.

Like I say I wasn't really part of that Spice Boys scene but I had my own period of madness with these guys when they invited me to go on a mini tour with them as a thank you for sorting the tickets.

I went to Cork in Ireland, Loch Lomond and they also played Maine Road, Manchester City's old ground.

It was a compete riot. I'd get to hang out with them backstage and got a front row seat to some of Liam's antics! It was an experience I'll never forget.

I loved having a chat with Noel after they'd performed. He knows his football and we'd have a good drink and a laugh talking about it.

I remember one time in Loch Lomond. The concert had finished and we were at an after show party. There were only a few of us there. I had a mate with me and there was also Noel, Liam, five of his pals and Patsy Kensit.

There was a lot of security and I was just kicking back with Noel talking football when Liam totally lost it.

He stood up screaming at Patsy. He picked up a plastic chair and smashed it against a wall. I was gobsmacked. It went very quiet for a moment before security piled in and chaos ensued.

They grabbed hold of Noel and whisked him away from the scene. Next thing I know they are doing the same with me and ushering us both into a car. It was a bit crazy. I don't know what happened after that but we finished up back in some hotel having a quiet drink. It was all a bit surreal.

Liam had a bit too much to drink after concerts. If you wanted to talk to him it would be best to have a chat within 10 minutes of a performance ending because he'd be off his face beyond that!

I was at the stage in my life where I was trying to cover up my worries about my career by having a great laugh off-the-pitch.

So, it's safe to say I wasn't expecting to meet my future wife when I was invited to judge a beauty contest with Louis Emerick at the David Lloyd Leisure Centre in Ellesmere Port.

Louis was famous for playing a character called Mick Johnson on the soap, Brookside.

I was happy enough to do it. After all, there are worse jobs than having to look at beautiful women trying to impress you for a few hours!

We were in the middle of a break in the proceedings when a small, attractive, dark-haired woman came over to Louis to give him a free membership.

I sat back waiting to be offered mine and surveyed the room.

When I turned back towards Louis she had gone.

He winked at me as if to say 'never mind mate.'

I wasn't bothered about the membership, it was just the fact that Mick off Brookside had been deemed more worthy a recipient than me!

A short while later the good-looking brunette appeared again. She looked rather tentative.

- Rob?

- Yes?

- I'm awfully sorry. I've just spoken to my manager who told me you play football for Liverpool. I should have offered you a membership. I didn't know who you were. Sorry about this but we'd like to give you a free membership too. My boss told me I had to apologise to you.

She looked sincere and slightly embarrassed.

I turned to her with an expression of mock disappointment.

- No, no... it's fine. I don't need a membership. Don't worry about it.

The brunette laughed and apologised again before disappearing into the crowd.

I had started to feel a little bit guilty that she may get into trouble with her boss, so when she returned I relented and accepted the free membership.

With the ice broken, I started to realise how much I was enjoying her company.

Her name was Sue and she had been a semi-professional tennis player. She'd been over to the USA and played at Flushing Meadow where she once trained with Andre Agassi.

I was intrigued and queried as to whether she was any good. She insisted that she had been but because of the vast amount of money you need to get started on the tennis circuit she had finally had to give up on her dream. Her parents had helped her so far, but in the end the cost of coaching, accommodation and the lifestyle in general proved too much. She'd returned to Cheshire and got a job working at the rackets.

I had been a keen tennis player in my teens and wanted to see if she had the talent to back up her story. So I challenged her to a showdown.

I kept teasing her in the pre-match warm up a few days later. I was saying that girls have no chance against lads. They just don't have the same power in the serve for a start.

She just kept smiling at me, nodding her head.

I continued to play the mind games, suggesting that I was bigger, faster and able to get around the court much easier.

Again she just smiled at me.

I suppose I should have realised that this was a sign of confidence but I really did think I would be too good for her.

I always remember that first serve. I can see it as clear as day even now.

She tossed the ball high into the air and arched her back before bringing her racket crashing through the centre of it.

A blur of yellow fizzed within inches of the net cord, crashed back up off the court and flew way beyond my belated swing.

'Ace,' she shouted with a jubilant laugh.

I was silent. I had barely moved. I told myself I would have to lose my over-confidence and prepared for the next service.

Unfortunately, it proved academic. She hammered me 6-0 in a one set match. I didn't even get a game off her!

My pride had taken a dent, but the defeat would go on to mark the start of our romance.

Within two years we married at the Chester Grosvenor. Unfortunately some of my Liverpool teammates couldn't make it due to their selection for the World Cup in France. But it was still an amazing day and the likes of Robbie, Bonus (Tony Warner), Harks, Craig Hignett and Roy were all in attendance. The Gaffer's wife even did a turn on the karaoke and put on quite a performance!

We're still happily married with three great kids. Natalie, Amy and Declan.

Natalie played hockey for Cheshire when she was at school and was also a bit of a star in the classroom, getting 9 A-grade GCSEs. She's now at the University of Manchester studying child psychology.

Amy is a very good netball player and has developed a real interest in horse riding. We are lucky enough to have land with space to keep horses and she has two Shetland ponies. It's a great hobby for her to have and she's won a few trophies for show jumping and the dressage.

Declan is our youngest. We thought we had best make one last effort to try and have a boy! Unsurprisingly he is an aspiring footballer and keeps asking me if he'll be good enough to turn professional. He's captain of his school's football team but I'm managing to keep his feet on the ground.

They have all followed in their parents' footsteps and done well at sport.

I like to think I'm still the top dog though and just for the record; I have since beaten Sue at tennis.

She doesn't play much with all of her work commitments so the gap in standard has been reduced considerably. We've got a tennis court in our back yard but she won't give me a regular game! She claims she gets too frustrated now. But it's only because I beat her most of the time.

CHAPTER NINE

Six years had elapsed and League Championship number 19 remained as elusive as ever.

I'd won a League Cup and an FA Cup during my time at Anfield but what I really wanted was to be part of a title-winning side.

Indeed, six years was far too long for Liverpool, but as the 1996-97 season gathered momentum there was a real credibility to our hopes of surpassing Manchester United as the best team in the land.

Our young side was a year older and many pundits were predicting that we would overcome our FA Cup final heartache and make a sustained challenge.

Frustratingly, I wasn't able to play my part. I was ruled out until the New Year and could only watch on as we made a superb start.

I had returned to Melwood in the autumn following a highly eventful rest period. The medical staff did another scan on my back and the fracture had healed.

I was delighted. I felt no pain and couldn't wait to start on the long trek back towards full fitness.

My absence had opened the door for Bjornebye to come in from the wilderness and make the left-wing back berth his own. He went on to have a sensational season and was named in the Premiership team of the year.

Jason continued to excel on the right hand side. I knew I had a real fight on my hands to get back in the team when I did eventually recover.

Roy also added to his backline with the free transfer signing of Bjorn Tore Kvarme. He came in and looked a real find to begin with so that meant competition was as stiff as ever.

It was a tough road back when I did finally return to training in the winter months. I had been out so long and it was very tentative at first. I had been told that my recuperation period had to be all about rest and so most of my time out was spent away from Melwood.

I felt I had done well the previous year and to be ruled out for so long was disappointing. The extent of the back injury concerned me too. Obviously thoughts that your career could be over filter through your mind at times like that and my focus was solely on getting back to fitness.

I've heard other players talk about how they have feared for their future at a club when their rivals have impressed in their absence, but that wasn't the case with me.

I didn't worry about how well Jason was doing or even Stig for that matter. I just wanted to be a part of it again. Watching the lads charge to the top of the table was really difficult and I was desperate to get back amongst the banter in the dressing room. Once I was fit again I knew it was up to me and I fully understood the need for Roy to bolster the squad.

Finally, after seven months of uncertainty, my comeback was pencilled in. A League Cup clash in Middlesbrough at the start of January. We had gone into the New Year clear at the top of the league and I was desperate to make an impact.

The doctor had told me I would be out until at least November, so I was chomping at the bit by the time the match at the Riverside came about.

I knew it would only be the start of an even bigger mountain to climb. There was still the small matter of match sharpness and that can take up to 10 matches after such a serious injury. Just look at the likes of Robbie and Michael Owen. They both had their problems and would often need a run of games to hit top form.

Unfortunately, it wasn't a good night for Liverpool. We went down to a 2-1 defeat and I played 75 minutes before being replaced by Jamie Carragher, who came on to make his debut.

You could see he had a real drive to make a career in the game. He's gone on to achieve massive things with Liverpool and is second in the all-time list of appearances for the club, which is no mean feat.

I think he's on record as saying Gerard Houllier played a major role in helping him to settle into the right lifestyle you need as a professional footballer. He's been incredible in over 15 years with the club and he's a great example to youngsters coming through the system.

He was more than happy to contribute to this book and was fantastic when I asked him if I could bring Declan up to Melwood to watch them train recently. He introduced him to Steven Gerrard and they were both great with us.

It's just one of those strange quirks of fate that saw him come on to begin his Liverpool odyssey at a time when mine was coming to an end.

Of course, I didn't know that then. I was still only 25 and convinced I had many, many years ahead of me at Anfield.

The Middlesbrough game would prove to be a false dawn.

It was just one of a mere three appearances I made that season. It was hard for my body to adjust to matches after being out for so long and with competition for places greater than ever, I struggled to force my way back in. There wasn't an issue with my back. That had healed. There were just little niggles here and there, not to mention the fact we were locked in a title race that meant there was probably a reluctance to alter a settled side.

Our Riverside defeat was also the start of what would be a difficult run-in to the season for Jamo. He was at fault for the first goal at Boro when his poor clearance led to my old Crewe roommate, Craig Hignett's opener.

He went on to have some dreadful moments which was a real shame because he had been one of our better performers in the first half of the season.

I don't know if we got January jitters but it was a torrid month. We managed just one league win and were dumped out of both the League Cup and the FA Cup. The latter was particularly galling as we were 2-0 up at the interval but went on to lose 4-2 at Chelsea.

I wasn't involved that day in London but the game sticks out as a potential turning point in our season.

We flew out to Amsterdam to play in a six-a-side tournament straight after the defeat and we were awful in that too. I don't think we won a game. It was all part of the celebrations and events organised to mark the opening of Ajax's new stadium.

It was then that cracks began to show. I remember Barnesy arguing with a few of the lads, suggesting some of their attitudes weren't right. There were fingers being pointed as to why we were suddenly taking beating after beating. There was a dark atmosphere that we were struggling to shake off and I think our results suffered.

We were still in the title race and started to pick up wins again after that trip but our form had definitely dipped.

The 4-3 win over Newcastle the previous season had been the stuff of legend and there was a real sense of euphoria following that win. But when lightning struck twice and Robbie popped up in stoppage time to clinch a success by the same scoreline this time around, all we felt was relief. We'd raced into a 3-0 lead but somehow let a patched up Magpies team back into it.

Jamo had a particularly tough evening. He took a lot of stick in the aftermath and the stories that his focus had been affected by his love of video games emerged. I think it's natural that everyone within a squad, from the coaching staff to the players, tend to analyse things and look for reasons to explain dips in form. I know Roy had noticed Jamo liked his video games and used to stay up until all hours playing them. He was concerned that it was stopping his number one goalkeeper from performing at his best. I don't know if addiction is the right word, but Jamo was always on them. If they weren't to blame then it was certainly a strange coincidence that his concentration suffered.

It put Roy in a tough position. As the mistakes piled up, our title challenge began to wane. A 3-1 defeat to Manchester United was a major blow and Jamo was seriously at fault for Andy Cole's second-half clincher.

We had Tony 'Bonus' Warner on the bench, who went on to have a good career, but I think Roy was reluctant to bring someone so inexperienced into the spotlight. Who knows if it would have made a difference?

We called Tony 'Bonus' because he always picked up the win bonus despite never getting off the bench! It was all good banter and I was made up that he showed just what he was capable of when he left Liverpool.

It was the same with Jamo. He was tarnished with the nickname 'Calamity James' and struggled to recover the form that saw him touted as one of the best goalkeepers in the country. It was only when he moved away from Anfield that he regained his confidence and went on to be massive for both England and the various clubs he represented.

Our season had promised so much, but any chance of a European Cup Winners' Cup final showdown with Bobby Robson's Barcelona evaporated when we put in a miserable display in a semi-final first-leg away to Paris St Germain. We lost 3-0 that night and although we gave it everything and could have hit double figures in the return game at Anfield, we only claimed a 2-0 triumph.

It meant the campaign ended in overall disappointment.

It was once again time to look towards the future. Our title hopes were mathematically ended by a 2-1 defeat at Wimbledon. It was a depressing night but one bright spot saw Michael Owen emerge from the bench to become the youngest player ever to score for Liverpool.

He was a breath of fresh air and had unbelievable pace. A few of the lads wanted to see him race me but we always used to laugh it off. They wanted a full-on 100m sprint!

He is a confident lad and I think most of the money would have been on him to win. I actually think I might have surprised them all.

I got on well with Michael. I used to travel in with him when he first burst onto the scene. He lived up by Hawarden and would drop his car off at my house before we headed to Melwood in mine.

He had a great career at Anfield and even won the Ballon d'Or, which is pretty special considering no other Liverpool player has achieved such an accolade.

Once he left L4 he never hit those heights again. He's just had injury after injury and the pace completely went. It started to go when he was at

Liverpool when he suffered all those issues with his hamstring. They tried all sorts with him. They even attempted to change the way he ran. He lost that turbo charge that used to get him away from defenders when he would knock it past them. If that's 80 per cent of your game, then you are going to dip.

It had been a shame to end the campaign without a trophy but on a personal level I was just happy to be back. Around February Roy had told me not to worry about being a regular in the line-up, and to make sure I was fit for the following season.

With that advice echoing in my mind, I went to David Lloyd leisure centre every day during the summer so that when I went back for pre-season, I was fit. I was back to where I had been in 95-96 and was right near the front of the pack in all of the training ground drills and races. I felt great.

I'd looked after myself all summer because I was eager to make sure I started the new season ready to fight for a place in the team. I was under no illusions; it was a massive campaign for me.

Once again we went into it thinking it would be our year. We had signed the leader everyone felt would give us the steel we were lacking in Paul Ince.

I was made up when we brought Incey in from Inter Milan. I knew him from England and was excited by what kind of player and person we were getting. I thought he'd be a great signing and he did okay. Maybe he didn't do as well as people hoped but he still made an impact during his time at Anfield.

I was delighted to begin the new campaign at right-wing back but as a team, we got off to an inconsistent start. After a 1-1 draw at Wimbledon we lost our first home match against Leicester City. We were really slow out of the traps and came in for some early criticism.

A lot of the press had made a big deal of a so-called battle of Britain, which had seen us drawn against Celtic in the UEFA Cup. It was a nice distraction from the domestic scene. We played the first-leg at Parkhead and looked to be slipping to a 2-1 defeat after Michael Owen had given us an early lead.

But when you have a player like Macca in your team you can never write yourself off completely. The game was heading towards stoppage time when he set off on one of those mazy runs. He just had an innate ability to glide beyond defenders that set him apart from many players. He scored the type of goal you usually see on the playground, slaloming beyond several challenges before curling home a sensational equaliser.

It was no secret that Macca made Liverpool tick. The 3-5-2 system we deployed gave him free reign just off the front two and if he was on song, we would rarely lose.

It hadn't gone unnoticed across Europe either. Macca had been a star of Liverpool's free-flowing side for the past few years and had also enjoyed a promising Euro 96 with England.

It was only natural that some of the continent's best teams would cast an admiring glance his way and after the Euros he was linked with a move to Barcelona.

Twelve months on and the rumours returned. I was a good friend of his and I still am so I knew that his contract was up the following summer. He'd made no secret of his desire to try his luck abroad. A lot has been written and said on the subject by fans and journalists alike, but the fact is that he alerted Liverpool to his intentions well in advance.

The Barcelona situation was all a smokescreen. They were after the Brazilian Rivaldo from Deportivo La Coruna and the deal had hit a snag.

As part of Barca's negotiating tactics, they moved for Macca in an attempt to twist Depor's arm. He flew over to Barcelona but then got a call to tell him that there would be no deal and that Rivaldo had completed a transfer to the Nou Camp.

Suggestions were mooted that Macca then made a decision to run down his contract after Liverpool had tried to offload him to Barcelona. That was utter rubbish.

I think Liverpool went on record to say that there had been no contact apart from in the August of 1996. That wasn't true.

His mum was seriously ill and he had let Liverpool know from the start that he wanted to leave. I think she had said to him to make the most of his life and experience everything it had to offer. He had always liked the idea of trying out a different culture and with the ordeal of dealing with his mum's illness, he just wanted a fresh start.

I don't think anyone could begrudge him that. He has always maintained that he informed Liverpool at a very early stage. However, the club told him that they would handle it and not to make his desire public.

Liverpool's official line was that Macca hadn't made his decision.

Things got more complicated when Gerard Houllier arrived the following summer but Macca didn't hide anything from him. Roy was already aware of the situation and Macca made sure Gerard was too.

I know some supporters think he was looking for the big pay day and left the club with nothing but that was never his intention. He would have preferred Liverpool to have received a fee for him. Don't forget, this is the club where he came through the ranks. He would have been more than happy to have seen them receive some reward for their efforts in nurturing his talents.

The whole saga wasn't handled well and in the January of 1999 he announced he had signed a pre-contract with Real Madrid. He had suffered with various knocks that season and his detractors were quick to assume it was because he was looking to keep himself free of injury prior to his big move.

Again, that wasn't quite true. His mother was terminally ill and on top of that he was burnt out from a non-stop football calendar. She died at the end of the season and I think the move away did him a great deal of good.

It's a real shame he's not regarded with the same sort of adulation as Robbie because he was up there with him as our best player in the 1990s.

He scored some great goals but he wasn't the most natural of finishers. I'd often be frustrated for him when he ended a slaloming 40 yard run with a weak back pass to the goalie. He was probably knackered by the time he came to shoot. But he didn't half score some crackers too. I saw a show on LFC TV dedicated to his best strikes the other day and a superb volley at Arsenal stood out. The shape of his body looked all wrong as he hit it, but it still flew into the top corner.

I think people forget just how good Macca was for Liverpool. The move to Real Madrid totally overshadowed all the great work that he did.

He went on to have a magnificent spell at the Bernabeu. He was underrated and didn't get the praise he deserved from the English press. He was appreciated in Spain and by his teammates but for some reason I don't think the recognition of his achievements were of the same level of someone like Beckham, who wasn't as successful at Madrid.

If the Celtic game had been the beginning of the end for Macca, it was significant to me for other reasons. It was the first time that I started to feel my knee. I didn't think much of it at the time but I was suffering with it throughout the match.

I missed the next three games but returned to start against Chelsea at Anfield. We won 4-2, thanks in no small part to a hat-trick from Patrik Berger. What may have gone unnoticed was that I had to be replaced at half-time by Jason. My knee was causing me real trouble again.

It began to really hamper me and I soon realised that playing back-to-back games was going to be a major issue. It was truly demoralising. I'd had so many injury woes over the years and always fought back. Now I had another problem that was preventing me from hitting a run of form and becoming a regular in the side.

I missed most of December and was on the bench for the majority of January until Jason broke his leg in a 0-0 draw at Blackburn Rovers.

Suddenly I was back in the thick of it all but I was finding it very tough. I was just getting through games rather than looking to make a positive impact.

At this stage of the season we had reverted to a 4-4-2 formation and I was playing in the right-back role where I had made my name. I was still producing decent performances but I knew I was well off the top of my game.

Our title bid had once again hit a brick wall and our hopes were all-but ended when Robbie picked up a serious injury in a 1-1 draw at home to Everton. He went up for a challenge with the goalkeeper Thomas Myhre and fell awkwardly. I could tell by his face that he knew something terrible had happened. To his credit, he tried to carry on and was limping about but in the end he just collapsed in agony.

It was a massive blow for both him and the club. It later emerged that he would face several months on the sidelines after tearing the cruciate ligament in his knee. It ruled him out of the 1998 World Cup finals in France, a big tournament heartache I was more than familiar with.

Robbie was never really the same player again. It's so easy to think that you can get your sharpness back. It took him so long. It was the same with me, but forwards seemed to come under the spotlight more. If you don't score then you aren't the same player. He did get it back in fits and starts for Liverpool but niggling injuries and a change in style to get the best out of Michael Owen meant he never hit his peak form.

There were signs when he left for Leeds that he would go on and prove Houllier wrong for selling him, but more injuries and the off-the-field financial problems that arose at Elland Road ultimately cost him.

I think he lost his spark when he was forced out of Liverpool that first time. He had grown up there and it was the only place he wanted to be.

When Rafael Benitez offered him the chance to come back in 2006 he couldn't sign the contract fast enough.

I thought that was an inspired piece of business and it was probably one of the best the Spaniard ever pulled off. Liverpool needed someone like that. I would watch games that were a bit dire and he would come on as a substitute. It would immediately give everyone a lift; both players and fans alike.

He did okay too. He scored a few goals for them and showed that he still had that ability to change games. I think they could still do with that, even now. They could wheel him out for the last 10 minutes of matches when the game needed a lift! I certainly wouldn't bet against him finding the net and winning a game or two, would you?

I know David Ngog has left now, but would you have rather have had him or Robbie coming on to rescue a game? I know who I'd choose every time.

Liverpool allowed Robbie to leave after Athens in 2007 but I think they could have kept him for a few more years. He'd have still done a job and think of the influence he could have had on younger players coming through. A player/coach role would have been ideal for him. It's a shame that didn't happen, but who is to say he won't return to Anfield again in a coaching capacity one day in the future. I know he'd love that.

It is an understatement to say that the summer of 1998 was a bleak one for Robbie, but I was facing my own crisis too.

The knee had troubled me all season and I was almost relieved when I played my final match of the campaign in a 4-1 defeat at Chelsea.

Jason returned from his broken leg after that and saw out the final few matches at right-back.

Little did I know that the disappointment at the Bridge would be my last ever appearance as a Liverpool player.

CHAPTER TEN

Michael Owen's stunning solo goal in England's World Cup clash with Argentina should have had me on my feet.

It was simply sensational and the type of strike that will go down in history as one of the greatest the competition has ever witnessed.

Who knows, if things had worked out differently I may well have been on the pitch there celebrating with him.

As it happened, I had to restrain myself while I punched the air on the sofa. I was surrounded by my mates, each one dancing a jig of joy. I swigged a bottle of beer and held on to my crutches, which were leaning on the armrest of a suite that was now vibrating as a makeshift drum.

'Eng- er-land, Eng - er -land'.

The thought of being part of Hoddle's England set-up hadn't really entered my mind. Once my knee had started playing up I knew that it would be a real battle to try and force my way into the squad. By the final few months of the season I was just desperate for it be over so I could get it sorted.

The initial medical advice was to rest. The doc had told me that I had patella tendonitis in my left knee. It had been flaring up during matches, swelling up in the hours after and then dying down after several days of R&R.

I was worried because I knew that my contract was up the following summer and I wanted to get a good pre-season under my belt so I could prove to Liverpool that I was still a player they could rely upon. They had offered me a new deal but it wasn't a fair one in my eyes.

The contract they had put forward was for three years and for exactly the same amount of money that I was already on.

I don't know if they offered it to me knowing that I wouldn't accept it, but after some negotiations it all stalled.

I wasn't being greedy. I just knew that the game had grown so much during that time and was hoping for a bit more.

I know I had endured problems with injuries over the years but I was disappointed by the offer and it did go through my mind that it could be time to make a move and have a fresh start.

But I was Liverpool through and through, so that was painful for me to contemplate.

In the end, I put the thought of a new deal to one side. An early operation was the order of the day and I went to see a specialist in Birmingham. He told me that the injury is often referred to as 'jumper's knee' because a lot of athletes tend to get it due to the impact they make when landing on hard surfaces.

I was optimistic I would make a full recovery but in the weeks that followed the surgery I knew that something wasn't right.

The specialist had told me that he had cut open my knee and scraped it clear. I didn't feel comfortable from that moment on and that has been the case to this very day.

I didn't know it at the time but other experts have told me that scraping the knee is the worst thing you can possibly do. I'm not going to say that all of my troubles would have gone away if they had got the first op right, but it certainly wouldn't have made things worse, that's for sure.

I tried to play a few games for the reserves when the season got underway but soon realised the operation had been unsuccessful. I started to work with Liverpool's medical team to try and find a specialist who had a successful history of dealing with this type of injury.

It was a very uncertain time for me.

The club had decided to bring in former France national team boss, Gerard Houllier during the summer to work alongside Roy as joint-manager.

It was a bizarre decision. Roy had turned Liverpool back into a force and we had been challenging for the title for the past three seasons.

None of the players understood it and I'd say 99 per cent of us were still right behind Roy and wanted him to lead our assault on the Premier League.

Roy himself was just bemused by it all. He had been such a fantastic servant to Liverpool for over 40 years and he wasn't about to cause a fuss. But maybe he should have? I felt it was disrespectful towards a man who had played an instrumental role in turning Liverpool into the club it was. He had been there, seen it and done it as far as our history of success was concerned.

I think the general reaction in the dressing room could be summed up as, 'what the fuck?'

It was almost like Houllier was a silent assassin. He merely observed things at first while Roy and the coaching staff took care of the day-to-day training sessions at Melwood.

It may have worked if they were best friends or a duo that had a tremendous understanding. But these two managers had never met each other before.

Right away it caused issues.

Who did you go to when you wanted to discuss your role in the team or ask why you weren't in the starting line-up last week?

I would always choose Roy because he was the one who had been my manager for several years and someone I trusted implicitly. I think that was the case for most of the lads.

I don't think that helped any of the 'old guard' with Houllier.

After a bright start results soon began to dip and the spotlight on the joint-managers intensified. There was only ever going to be one winner and after a League Cup defeat at home to Tottenham, Roy resigned.

I know he felt let down by the club and their distinct lack of faith in him.

From a personal point of view, it was a disaster.

I knew that I wasn't Houllier's cup of tea and that I was probably going to be a part of his clear out. Liverpool had signed the Norwegian full-back Vegard Heggem during the summer and my route back into the first-team appeared to be even more unlikely.

Of course, Roy was involved in that decision too.

'Veggie' was the only signing made by the joint managers. He'd scored a famous winner for Rosenborg against AC Milan and was a highly-rated attacking right-back.

I think Jason was more put out by the transfer than I was. I'd been struggling with injury so much that I accepted that the club needed reinforcements. If I wasn't going to be fit they needed to find someone who would be.

But my relationship with Houllier was non-existent. It was a problem from day one.

It was like being at school again with a new headmaster who was obsessed with rules and discipline. It was clear he was trying to make a statement and I think the power went to his head a little bit.

We'd always had a great camaraderie under Roy but the atmosphere suffered under Houllier.

He came into the treatment room one day and told me my problems were all in my head and if I got back out on the training pitch I would realise there was nothing wrong with me.

I told him that was so far from the truth it was laughable and that I would love nothing more than to go out and join the lads doing the drills. He left the room exasperated and I felt pretty low.

A few days later I opened up the paper to see that he had done an interview with the Press in which he claimed all of my injury problems were in my mind and that I was 'acting' injured.

I was furious.

We had showdown talks where he again insisted that I listen to him and just attempt to train instead of moping about in the treatment room.

Reluctantly I agreed.

When I did try to venture out onto the training pitch I immediately broke down again. I was left crumpled in a heap, cursing him for having such little time to listen to what I was actually saying.

When he heard I was going for a second operation just a few months into the new season, the offer of a new contract was withdrawn.

I knew I needed to find someone who had experience of performing successful surgery on the specific problem I had. We eventually found a Dr Barrett who was willing to take a look at me.

He was a specialist who was based down in Southampton. He was the one who told me that you should never scrape it like the first surgeon had. Once you do that, you rip the top of the tendons and it'll never grow back. It results in a lot of scar tissue.

He performed the keyhole surgery on my knee and although it felt better for a short period after the operation, I inevitably broke down again.

He even tried to take a bit of my knee cap away as he felt it was catching the top of the tendons. Again, it worked for a bit but in the end I was just pulling up in agony.

It's a strange injury because in the majority of cases, players will take anti-inflammatory tablets and have an injection that would mean they would be okay within four weeks.

However, with the likes of myself, Owen Hargreaves and the Brazilian Ronaldo it just didn't heal.

I suppose it's a good example of how a footballer's dreams can be crushed as a contract comes to an end.

I've often spoken to Macca about it. I'm left without a contract because of injury and have to seek out another club to continue my career, while on the other side of the spectrum he played out the last year of his contract and moved to Real Madrid on a good deal.

I think if Roy had still been in sole charge there may have been a possibility that Liverpool would have kept me on. I'm not saying they would have given me the deal. I had a crippling knee injury. But I think Roy would have told me to return the following pre-season after my contract had run out and try to get my knee right.

I don't think it would have been 'see ya' like it was with Houllier.

I suppose his decision was vindicated because I did finish. I can't argue with that but I think Roy had a bit more class. He would have recognised that I'd given Liverpool good service. He'd have offered me the chance to try and prove I could still do it. If that hadn't worked out, it wouldn't have done Liverpool, Roy or myself any harm.

By the February of 1999 I knew that my Liverpool career was well and truly over.

I was playing for the reserves in a match at St Helens' rugby league ground and could feel the pain throbbing in my knee. I was running with gritted teeth and knew my concentration on the game was being affected.

'Why isn't this going away?'

The words echoed in my mind every time my studs impacted on the turf, causing a searing pain to engulf my knee cap.

Every now and then I would hear the angry bark of Sammy Lee on the touchline, furious that I had once again pulled out of a 50-50 challenge.

I just didn't want people to know that I was back to square one. Again.

I had returned for another scan a month after the second operation and once more it had shown an inflammation.

I could feel Sammy glaring at me in the dressing room after the game. I didn't want to catch his eye.

As I headed out to the team bus I spoke to the physio and told him that my knee was knackered.

I sat at the back of the coach on my own. I could feel the devastation beginning to overwhelm me. I had fought it off after the match but now that I was alone I gave in to the emotion.

I picked up the phone and rang Sue. When she answered I just burst into tears. I was completely incoherent so I just hung up.

The lads started to filter onto the bus and saw that I was in a state. They tried to have a bit of banter with me and told me everything would be okay.

As the coach pulled away from the ground my phone rang.

It was Macca.

Sue must have made some sense of what I was saying and decided that he was the best one to talk to me. He told me not to let it beat me. He said he would support me as much as possible and that it would all work out, that I just needed to be strong.

The next day at Melwood, I told the doc that I wanted to have a third operation and attempt to get fit in time for the pre-season so I could try and impress a potential new club.

When the realisation hit me that I was finally leaving Liverpool it knocked me for six. I'd had it in the back of my mind and had spoken to family and friends about it, but I don't think I truly thought it would happen.

The idea that I would no longer be Rob Jones of Liverpool Football Club raised a lump in my throat.

I'd always been firmly committed to the cause and never considered a transfer. I'd had informal approaches but always rebuffed them straight away.

I remember Peter Beardsley came up to me during a meet-up with the England squad back in 1993. He was just chatting about life in general when all of a sudden he mentioned that Kevin Keegan had been asking about me. He had told Peter to speak to me and see if I'd be interested in a move to Newcastle. I stopped him right in his tracks. I was a Liverpool fan and it had been my boyhood dream to play for them. Why on earth would I want to leave? It's nice to hear that other clubs and their managers appreciate your qualities as a footballer but like I say, it was Liverpool all the way for me.

Now, it was no longer my choice. Liverpool didn't want me so I had to look to pastures new.

The third operation had also been unsuccessful and I knew that I was running out of options. I needed to find another club and convince them to take a chance on me.

There were a few that were interested. I spoke to Blackburn boss Brian Kidd on the phone and there was some interest from Glasgow Rangers too. But nothing came of the contact from either club.

I didn't really have an agent so there was no one out there touting my name to other teams. The summer was fast approaching when both Redders and his brother, Mark suggested that their Dad, Harry, might be interested in taking me to West Ham.

I spoke to Harry and he was great. He told me he would sort the deal out and that all I had to do was prove my fitness. There was a five-year contract on the table with a substantial wage, *if,* I could stay fit and show that my knee problems were behind me.

The Hammers had a talented young squad with the likes of Frank Lampard, Joe Cole and Rio Ferdinand in the set-up. There was also Paolo Di Canio, Ian Wright and my old Liverpool teammate, Neil Ruddock.

It wasn't just the contract that appealed to me. I could see they were a team that liked to play attacking football. I knew that if I could get a run in the side at right back there was always a chance that I would be involved with England once again.

I spoke to Sue about it and told her that if I was going to join West Ham then we would all have to move down south. I didn't want to be one of those players who lived in a hotel room and commuted back and forth at different times throughout the week. If I was going to do it, then I was going to give it my all to be a success and that started with getting the family settled.

As ever, Sue was tremendously supportive and within days I was clearing out my locker at Melwood.

It was set up to be a poignant moment but proved to be a bit of an anti-climax. You expect it to be a defining moment for you, one that remains with you for the rest of your days.

What would the lads say to me? Would they give me a big send off?

I didn't know what to expect. How would I handle running into Houllier?

I needn't have worried. It was a very quiet and short experience.

I'd been training by myself for a few weeks so most of the players had either gone on their summer holidays or set off for international duty.

I glanced around the locker room that had been a huge part of my life for so long.

This was it.

The end.

A few dinner ladies and some physios were the last faces I saw as I made a lonely exit into the car park.

I started the engine and paused for the briefest of moments.

No, this wasn't a bad dream. This was now my reality.

I put the car into gear and rolled towards the gate where a dozen or so loyal supporters would often congregate to get a glimpse of their heroes and chance a quick autograph.

Not today.

There were no witnesses as I waved to the security staff and drove out of Melwood for the final time as a Liverpool player.

It was a sad moment but one that made me even more determined to prove everyone wrong and make it work down in London.

CHAPTER ELEVEN

I can remember the first day at Chadwell Heath vividly.

I'd been waiting for the moment ever since I pulled out of the Melwood gates and was desperate to impress.

It had been a frustrating month or so. I had hoped to spend most of it in the gym, getting myself as fit as possible before joining up with Harry and the lads. But my knee kept swelling whenever I attempted any vigorous exercise and I spent the majority of the time resting it.

The first person to greet me when I arrived was Harry. He's such an enthusiastic character and makes you feel right at home straight away. He told me he was delighted to have me on board.

I got there early. I was over-eager in many ways and there were just one or two of the younger lads in the changing room when Harry took me down to meet everyone.

I shook a few hands and realised my palms were sweaty. I was nervous. I'd been at Liverpool and played alongside some of the biggest names in the game but it's still nerve-wracking when you are the new boy.

Harry told me to choose a 'peg' where I could lay out my kit and make myself at home. I glanced around the empty room and opted for a spot in the corner, out of the way.

Harry burst out laughing.

-That's Wrighty's seat. You know what he's like. Might be an idea to choose another one.

I had to smile. It would have been typical if I'd chosen former Arsenal striker, Ian Wright's seat. He is as bubbly a character as you will come across and would undoubtedly have taken great pleasure in teasing me in front of the other lads.

My mind flashed back to my first few days with Liverpool and when I poured water all over McMahon's food. It seemed I was destined to mark myself out as memorable right from the outset.

I decided to move along one but when I heard Ian coming down the corridor I quickly shifted back into his seat. I knew him well from being in several England squads together and thought he'd help settle some of my jitters with a bit of banter.

His face was a picture when he walked in. Mock outrage was followed by a big handshake and a pat on the back. He made sure everyone was introduced to me and put me at ease immediately.

I started to get a good vibe about the place. As I witnessed the lads having a laugh I began to feel like I could make a real go of it. Harry had nurtured a great spirit there.

Unfortunately, training was a different matter. Pre-season is all about running and that isn't good for someone with a dodgy knee.

We did two sessions a day to begin with and it was causing me some real aggro.

My life was all about hotel, running, hotel, food and then bed. I was permanently exhausted and I couldn't shake the nagging pain in my leg either.

It was all very repetitive, but my sole focus was on getting myself fit to sign that contract.

I felt a real pressure. I was still only 27 and had a family of four to support. I felt like I was going under the microscope to prove to West Ham that I wasn't a gamble. Looking back I was just lying to myself.

Sue had quit her job to make the move with me and she was based at the hotel with Amy who was still a baby at the time. Natalie had remained with Sue's parents, Bernie and Mike, because she still had school.

She came down to visit us at weekends while I tried to get the contract that would see us permanently up sticks to the capital.

We were in a state of limbo and I think the only one who was enjoying it was Amy.

She was two years old and was having a ball using the hotel swimming pool. She actually learned to swim there and was establishing herself as a big hit with the staff. She was tottering up and down the corridors saying hello to everyone. She was a bit of a star.

Meanwhile, I was doing everything I could to get myself fit and ready for action but the knee was just a mess. I realise that now and see that the pressure came from a subconscious acceptance of that. It was a fear I was unwilling to face at the time in case I got the answer I didn't want to hear.

The fact that I managed to complete a full pre-season only enhanced my delusion that everything was going to be fine.

If I had just been suffering with niggling injuries and needed to prove to West Ham that I was a decent footballer, I wouldn't have felt any pressure. I had faith in my ability.

The prospect of a five year deal with such a good wage was also far too enticing. I wasn't looking beyond that. It was all about convincing people I was fine. And it was clear that I wasn't.

I was midway through a pre-season game when Harry called me over to the dugout.

- You do realise you are limping when you try to run, don't you?

- No. I'm not. I just picked up a bit of a dead leg in that tackle earlier.

-Are you sure you're okay?

- I'll be fine. I'll run it off.

When I came off the pitch my knee had ballooned. I was spending half of my time icing it after training and it was the same again at night.

West Ham had insisted that I prove myself over three months. If I came through that period then the contract was mine.

I had become obsessed by it. I wanted it so badly. I didn't want my career to be over.

We played an Intertoto Cup match in Norway and once again I was battling through the pain barrier. Eventually I had to concede defeat and hobbled off clutching my knee in agony.

It was full of fluid and both the physio and the doctor decided to take samples to see what could be done.

When the results came back I knew what they would say, so I made an appointment to see the specialist in Southampton. After the scan he told me that he would do another operation but that there would be no guarantees.

Things were far worse than I had imagined. My articular cartilage had worn away. My knee was now so weak that there was no hope. I was told that I wouldn't be able to train every day and there was no way it would hold up to the rigours of the Premier League.

The surgeon did one final operation. Not only did he focus on the patella tendon, but he had to drill some holes into my bone just to let the fluid out.

I was devastated.

I phoned Sue and told her the news. She tried her best to comfort me but what could she say? This was all that I had known. It was such a big part of my life and all of a sudden it was gone. I felt like someone had died.

I was dreading making the call to Harry. He'd been so good to me and I knew that I had been deceiving him a bit over the past few weeks as I tried to get the contract.

It may sound like I was trying to pull the wool over everyone's eyes and that I wasn't doing the right thing. But that wasn't the case at all. Up until the last appointment with the surgeon I thought I could do a job for West Ham. I may not have been a regular but I thought that if I could just get the contract signed I could then focus on getting the knee right. It may seem stupid to sign a contract and then sit on the sidelines for a bit but when you are faced with no-win situations you are willing to clutch at any hope at all.

Harry was brilliant with me. He was genuinely upset that I couldn't sign the deal. He said that if it had been up to him he would have given me a contract and helped me as much as possible in my rehabilitation. But it was down to the board and they were just doing what was best for West Ham.

I felt numb.

I couldn't digest much of what was going on around me and it was only later that I truly appreciated what everyone did for me.

I had been in London for almost two months with no pay. I was staying at a nice hotel with my family and the bill was on the large side. It wasn't an ideal situation but then Harry stepped in and insisted on paying for everything. That was a fantastic touch. I'll always be grateful to him for that and for giving me the chance to try to resurrect my career.

Sadly, my only option now was to retire. As the news broke that I was hanging up my boots at the age of 27, I decided to stay down in London and take some time to come to terms with it all. We had sold our houses in the north west and were effectively homeless, so another week or two in the capital wasn't going to harm us.

The West Ham boys all rallied around me. They were brilliant. My old Liverpool teammate, Neil Ruddock called me up and took me out for a few beers. John Moncur, Trevor Sinclair and Steve Lomas were also great and they organised a big night out. It was a nice gesture, even if I was enjoying it on crutches.

Eventually it was time to face up to it all.

We headed back to Cheshire with no home to lay our heads. We ended up staying at Sue's parents' house for six months as we looked to sort out a new place to live.

It was brilliant of them to welcome us into their home. I will never forget their support but at the time I felt embarrassed and even more depressed. I was a Premier League footballer living with my partner's mum and dad. It certainly wasn't where I expected to be at 27.

The great West Ham hope had lasted all of six weeks. I had signed non-contract terms in the middle of July so that I was eligible to play in the Intertoto Cup but was forced to pack it all in on August 28, 1999.

In total I had endured six operations on the knee but in the end nothing could be done to save my career.

In the weeks and months that followed I received calls from a lot of the lads. Redders, Macca, Incey and Michael Thomas were particularly good with me and tried to get me out of the house.

But I wasn't much company. I felt helpless and didn't know what to do with myself.

I had no idea what the future held but in my darkest moments I did wonder if the best years of my life were already gone.

CHAPTER TWELVE

Silence was once again my companion as I buried my head under the duvet.

The distant chatter of Sue getting Natalie and Amy ready for school and nursery had long since passed. I was left alone with my thoughts.

The roar of the Kop, Ronnie Moran's fierce expression and the lads enjoying some dressing room banter were all images that swirled within my head. It had been a recurring theme throughout the first few months of my 'retirement'.

I had hoped it would be different. I prayed I would wake up with a new sense of wellbeing that would see the second stage of my life begin.

But when I opened my eyes and looked up at the blank, mundane paintwork of the ceiling, I still felt the same as I had the previous morning. It was all gone.

Nothing prepares you for life after football. You hear players who hang their boots up at the age of 37 talking about how they struggled to adapt to the world outside the unique bubble of a Premier League squad.

Well, imagine what it's like at 27.

It's supposed to be your peak. The period when all of your potential is finally fulfilled and you hit the prime of your career.

All of these thoughts return like an unwelcome guest as you drag your body into the shower and feel the warmth of the hot water attempting to spark you into life. It used to do the trick.

You sit at the breakfast table and try to put on a brave face in front of your wife. You share a joke and enjoy each other's company, but it's not the same as that buzz you get from arriving at Melwood every day.

The routine was gone. The smiles and the laughter of the dressing room - gone. It's hard to accept that the day-to-day banter is over forever.

That's when you feel down. You don't know what to do with yourself.

Matters were made worse by the fact we were still living with Sue's parents.

It's fair to say that life wasn't too good.

I thought of Macca at Real Madrid and how he was starting an incredible new adventure. I was finished, a washed up crock hoping to find a new path in life. He was on the verge of mega-stardom with arguably the biggest club on the planet.

You couldn't have blamed him if he had focused on that and got in touch with me a few months later. But that wasn't Macca. He was thinking of me and probably realised how hard it would be.

Next thing I know he is on the phone and is telling me he has booked me on a flight to Madrid.

The shock sent a wave of adrenalin pumping through my veins. Before I knew it, there was an extra spring in my step and the smile was back on my face.

Sue was relieved to see a bit of the old me had returned and was more than happy to see me head off to the airport.

Little did I know that my first day in the Spanish capital would see me at the heart of a massive celebration dinner amongst the entire Real squad. When Macca arrived to pick me up he explained that one of the lads had just had his first baby and that the team were going out to celebrate. He had only just joined and barely spoke a word of Spanish but was determined to go along and show he was keen to be a part of the group.

I think that's why he had such a good relationship with his teammates throughout his time at Real. In those early days he would still turn up and get involved even though his Spanish was limited.

So there am I, stood in Madrid airport being told that I was going to be his guest at this massive celebration. He phoned the France international, Christian Karembeu, who spoke a bit of English to confirm whether it was okay that I attend. It wasn't a problem.

It was a bit nerve-wracking to be honest. We arrived at a restaurant in town and sat at a long table. I was sandwiched between Fernando Hierro and Ivan Campo. Macca was opposite me. There were mega stars everywhere I looked. It was a bit of a buzz and somewhat daunting at the same time.

I started chuckling to myself when the glasses were chinked and all eyes turned on Macca. It was his first informal get-together with his new teammates and part of the initiation was to stand up and give a speech. Rather him than me, I thought to myself.

There were a couple of new boys there that night so he wasn't alone. Macca had to do his in Spanish and he managed to say a few words without making a fool of himself.

I thought that would be the end of it but an uneasy feeling began to surface in the pit of my stomach when a rapid exchange in Spanish was followed with Macca nodding and looking at me.

I could sense it coming. I pulled a face and gave Macca a subtle shake of my head. He just smirked. He could just about understand what they were saying.

He leaned towards me.

- Trig mate. You're going to have to get up and give a speech.

- You're kidding aren't you?

- Come on mate, it's only a bit of fun. You'll be fine.

- Macca, I can't speak a word of Spanish. I'm just going to look like an idiot.

- It's okay. They are happy for you to do it in English. And besides, there are only a couple of people on the entire table who will understand what you are saying. Easy mate.

So there I was, stood like a complete lemming speaking to a table of superstars. Needless to say, I had necked a few beers for Dutch courage a moment or two before my brief cameo in the Madrid spotlight!

I kept it short and sweet. I congratulated the player on the birth of his new baby and thanked them for inviting me. No one seemed to know what on earth I was saying and there were a few seconds of awkward silence before Macca burst out laughing. That gave the others the cue to join in and there were a few slaps on the back for me.

I figured that they all just assumed I was a nobody from England who was big pals with Macca but I later found out some of them knew who I was.

I went to the toilet and Hierro came and stood next to me at the sink when we were washing up.

- You. You were Liverpool. Right-back, no?

I was a bit taken aback but I was made up he was trying to speak to me.

- Yes, that's right. Not anymore but I used to be at Liverpool.

- Ah, I thought so. I said to Macca that I knew your face.

He walked off wagging his finger at me and smiling.

When I got back to the table word had begun to spread. There were quite a few cheers for me as I sat down and when I caught the eye of the likes of Raul and Roberto Carlos there were a lot of smiles and nods.

It turned out to be a great night and was the perfect pick me up.

I returned to Madrid six months later and when I came through the arrivals gate, Macca started laughing.

-You pick your times mate. The lads are having a night out tonight. It's the first one since you were here last time! You're going to have to come again.

They were a good bunch. Macca later told me that they actually thought I was living with him! They assumed that because I kept turning up at the get-togethers I must be based in Madrid.

I'm just glad they didn't think I was his partner!

I had some amusing adventures visiting El Macca.

If it wasn't hobnobbing with Galacticos, it was watching him try to convince the Spanish police I wasn't an intruder after setting off his garage alarm in the early hours one morning!

Macca's wife, Victoria, had been involved in a minor road accident that had left the side of her car badly scratched.

I had woken up early the next morning and decided to make myself useful by trying to tidy it up before she took it in for repairs.

I found what I *thought* was the garage door remote control on the kitchen table and ventured outside into the Madrid sunshine.

I hit the button a few times expecting the door to slowly creak open.

Nothing.

I hit it again and again, hoping it would suddenly kick into life.

Silence.

I examined it more closely, wondering if the batteries had died.

I moved closer to the door and tried pressing the buttons from various angles. It didn't budge.

I was about to give up and head back inside when the faint sound of sirens cut through the silence in the yard.

They appeared to be heading in my direction and I began to think that one of Macca's neighbours may have been burgled.

I ventured towards his security gate to have a quick scout around.

Nothing appeared out of the ordinary.

Suddenly the noise filled the street and three police cars screeched to a halt in a blur of flashing blue.

A couple of officers leapt out and started shouting at me in Spanish.

I was stunned. I didn't know what to say.

I tried to explain that I was a guest of Macca's but they were equally baffled by my English.

They appeared to repeat their initial comments in Spanish, but this time there was more intensity in their tone.

I began to get a little bit concerned.

They motioned for me to raise my hands and I gestured that it wasn't necessary.

It wasn't looking good until the front door opened and a tired-looking Macca appeared.

He spoke in fluent Spanish with a smile that immediately put the police at ease.

It transpired that I had picked up the remote control for a panic alarm and I had caused a real stir at Madrid HQ with my repeated button-pressing!

As the police drove away from a memorable false alarm, Macca shook his head at me and laughed. I guess he was used to me getting myself into trouble.

I never did get around to having a look at Vicky's car. She probably thought she'd be better off taking her chances with the mechanics after my struggles with the garage door!

I was delighted with the success Macca had at Madrid. Some people have suggested he was only signed by Madrid because he was on a 'Bosman' and they could make a profit from selling him, but he showed everyone at the Bernabeu just how good a player he was.

He scored a fantastic goal in the 2000 Champions League final and was named man of the match. I was his guest that night in Saint-Denis and I was buzzing for him.

Those visits to Madrid were massive in helping me come to terms with life after football.

When I got home following my second trip to Madrid I wanted to make a big effort and stop moping around.

I'd had a phone call from Mark Wright who was the manager at Southport. He asked me if I'd be interested in playing in the non-league for him.

Your initial instinct is to say yes, but after mulling it over I came to the conclusion that nothing had changed. My knee wouldn't have been able to cope with it. I'd just about survived six months of heartache after having to give up the sport professionally, so I didn't want to have to go through it all again if my body couldn't live up to the demands.

I know my old teammate, Mike Marsh played for a good few years in non-league after initially retiring through injury. He made a real success of it.

There is a rule that you can't play in the football league if you have a pay-out through your injury insurance. Wrighty knew that I had been struggling without the game but it was never really on the cards and I had to make a decision about what I was going to do next.

I sat down with Sue and she agreed that it was time for me to start focusing on the future. We spoke about what would interest both of us.

We came up with different ideas, but it was a problem we were encountering in our home life that provided us with a 'light bulb' moment.

We'd noticed that the area around Warrington where we had recently moved, didn't have many nurseries. We needed childcare at different times of the week and we were struggling to find places. We'd identified seven in total but they were all fully booked.

That's when we thought that it might be an option to try and open up our own.

We continued to think of different ventures we could start but we just kept coming back to children's nurseries. Since having the kids Sue had always taken an active interest in the nurseries anyway and after doing some sums we thought that it could well be a project that would suit both of us.

So off she went to college to get the necessary qualifications while I went around the local area looking at properties that could be suitable for us to renovate.

I had received a decent amount of money from my insurance pay out and I'd also been quite prudent with what I had earned throughout my career. You hear about some players who squander a month's wages on a night out or at the bookies. I wasn't like that.

Thankfully, it meant we had a bit of money set aside that would help us to make the first step.

After looking at several places I found one in Stockton Heath.

That was in early 2001. Sue was heavily pregnant with Declan at that point but it didn't stop her getting everything in place before he arrived in the March.

We called the business 'The Kids Academy Nursery Group' and it proved to be a massive success.

Macca had given me a signed Zidane shirt and I stuck that, along with a few others he had sent me, up on the walls for decoration. Not that the kids took much notice. It's not really something that impresses a two-year-old!

We had a bit of a launch party the day we opened the first nursery and it was nice to see some of my sporting friends hadn't forgotten me.

Robbie, Barnesy and Danny Murphy were all in attendance, as was the sprinter Darren Campbell.

It did so well that we were able to expand the business by opening another nursery that we called 'The Stables.' We eventually sold the first one but we still own 'The Stables'.

With the profit we made from that sale we expanded again and bought more and more nurseries. We've continued to fill them and the business has flourished.

We opened the Kalgarth Grange Day nursery on Manchester Road and the 117 places we had available were filled almost overnight. We realised there was still a massive demand and in late 2010 we succeeded in obtaining a bank loan that meant we were able to increase the capacity so we could take in 50 additional children.

Most, if not all of the credit must go to Sue. She's been the one who has learned everything about nurseries from a business point of view and she has ensured that we have stayed ahead of the game.

She has kept up to speed with all of the changes in child care over the past 10 years. You have to look at all levels of security including CCTV, not to mention a changing curriculum.

We've added breakfast, holiday clubs, a lift service to and from the nursery, as well as mum and parenting classes. It's all about catering for what the community wants and Sue is brilliant at ensuring our nurseries meet all of the demands.

We are very proud of what we have achieved with them. The Willows in Warrington's town centre has been particularly good and was given an 'outstanding' report by Ofsted.

I was heavily involved when we first started out but Sue is in full control now. She's the one who looks after the day-to-day running of things.

It was what needed to happen really because the pressure of operating a popular business where the demand was increasing beyond what we initially had in terms of man power, inevitably caused a bit of strain on us.

Don't get me wrong. It wasn't harming our marriage. We just felt that it was making life harder for us and we wanted to keep the business and our personal life separate. The easiest way to do that was for me to take a step back once we had the staff and the necessary means at our disposal.

That was around two years into the project.

My role from that moment on has been to take charge of investment. It's suited both of us down to the ground and the business has grown beyond our wildest dreams.

We've been able to branch into care homes as well and in the last few years it's taken a really exciting twist.

We received a phone call out of the blue from some people saying they were representatives of Khalifa Bin Hamoodah.

The Bin Hamoodah Company is one of the world's richest business empires and is based in the United Arab Emirates. They have interests in a number of sectors, including oil and gas, food, IT and real estate, to name but a few.

It transpired that the family were eager to make a commitment to education in their country and wanted to know more about the Kids Academy Nursery Group. They want to provide the ultimate in terms of childcare, so they can give something back to their community.

I don't know how they came across our business, but it's fantastic that they have and that they were eager to know more.

The initial contact was all via Sue and I didn't get involved until she came home in a flurry of excitement one evening saying that they wanted to fly us out there to discuss expanding our nurseries to the UAE.

It was huge news and a massive mark of the respect the business has gained since it first started. We were all really excited about what it could mean for our future.

We weren't about to get ahead of ourselves, but we realised that it could lead to a whole new life.

So, one rainy Monday morning at Manchester airport, off we went, ready for another adventure.

If you've never been to Abu Dhabi before, then I can assure you it is quite breathtaking. They like to do things 'big' over there and they tend to do it with a lot of money and a lot of style.

We were treated like royalty from day one. Nothing was too much trouble and everything was complimentary.

I was really enjoying my time there but became slightly wary of our impending meeting when his PA arrived to brief me about how I should conduct myself.

The culture over there is very different and you must respect it at all times.

Sue had already met him and she had warned me that he would not indulge in too much conversation.

It meant a pocket of apprehension had built up in my stomach prior to arriving at the restaurant where the meeting was scheduled. I didn't want to ruin anything for Sue or cause any offence and kept running through what I could and couldn't do.

Of course, I needn't have worried.

After I'd had a couple of beers, I loosened up and we had a great laugh. I had just started writing this book at the time and told them what I was up to.

I expected them to take a real interest because everywhere you go in the world, it seems Liverpool FC has an army of followers.

But as it turned out, they weren't actually that keen on football. I suggested getting a few of the former Liverpool lads over there to help launch the nurseries; again, thinking they would be very interested.

But they explained to me that footballers aren't seen as superstars in their country. If they launch a new project or hold a party they tend to have people like U2 playing to a small audience or get Britney Spears or Paul McCartney out there.

I have to say, I liked the idea of Bono giving a special live performance to a select group to mark the opening of our first nursery in Abu Dhabi! Or maybe we could get Oasis back together, just for old time's sake!

As it turned out, there was no such fanfare when our inaugural nursery opened in the January of 2012.

We've had some fantastic reports about its progress and Khalifa and his associates have reiterated their desire to see us make a move to the UAE on a permanent basis.

We've become good friends and I've even managed to convince him that football is worth watching. He's a big Liverpool fan now and I even presented him with a signed shirt the last time we were out there.

It's great that they have such faith in us.

The Bin Hamoodah group have now bought the franchise for our nurseries and they plan to open 20 in the UAE in the next five years alone. There are also discussions that this could expand further into

Qatar, Saudi Arabia, Bahrain and Turkey. It will basically cover the whole of the middle east, which is absolutely huge.

It's mindboggling for us really, but we are trying to stay grounded. If it does take off as planned then I must admit we would consider relocating. Abu Dhabi is a brilliant place to be and the lifestyle is fantastic.

I'll have to make sure I'm fully up to speed with all of the customs though. I had a bit of fright when we went to Dubai on holiday last year.

It was Sue's 40th birthday and as part of her present I flew us all over there for a break in the sun.

You'd think I would be on the ball when it comes to security procedures in airports when you consider how much I go away with Liverpool's legends, but on this occasion I was caught out.

I was looking forward to a cold beer by the pool and was already impatient to get to the chauffeur collecting us when I noticed Natalie was lagging behind.

I hung back and waited for her. She finally got to the security desk but I saw her face drop when they started to call more officers over.

I dashed forward to see what the problem was.

They had found a bullet in her bag.

No wait, it was *my* bag.

We had been scurrying around the house trying to make sure we had enough cases for all of us and I had dug out an old green sports bag that I hadn't used for a few years.

I realised straight away that I had last used it on a trip to Scotland when I had gone shooting.

I took the sport up as a bit of a hobby about five years ago. Most ex-pros choose to play golf, but I developed a real buzz for shooting. I suppose it's a bit ironic, given my shooting record as a footballer! I can assure you my aim is a little bit better than it was at goal!

Anyway, I quickly explained the situation and hoped we could resolve it without too much fuss.

When they pulled out the handcuffs and escorted me away, I realised I was in a bit of trouble.

I was interviewed for two hours in a small room on the lower floors of the airport. I was asked the same questions by two different police officers and I continued to detail what had happened.

I don't know whether they thought I was planning something awful or what, but it didn't seem to convince them. After what felt like an eternity I was moved again. This time I was taken upstairs to an actual cell.

I could see the headlines. Former Liverpool star banged up abroad. You think you'd have more concern about your safety at this point, but I couldn't help think that the lads would have a field day with this one when they found out about it. I guess that's what years of being part of a dressing room does to you.

Another four hours dragged by as I paced up and down in my own private hell. I started to think that I was never getting out when a senior officer appeared. He had a cluster of impressive medals attached to his chest and seemed to command immediate respect from those around him.

He asked the same question again. Why had I brought a bullet into the country?

Once more, I offered my version of the events.

I was completely exasperated and wondered how many times I'd have to say it.

He pulled out a form and handed me a pen.

I asked him what it said but he just told me to sign it.

I wasn't happy. It could have said anything. You always hear about these horror stories in foreign prisons and I could have been admitting to anything by putting pen to paper on that.

It was his turn to become frustrated. Impatiently he tapped the form.

Finally, after a few moments of deliberation I put my signature on it. I was immediately released and taken back to my family.

Apparently Sue had become so worried she had burst into tears, prompting a gentleman in traditional Arabic dress to enquire what was wrong. She explained what had happened and he had sought to resolve it. It was he who had approached me with the form. He was the man responsible for my release.

I still don't know what the form said and I haven't heard anything since. It hasn't stopped me returning to the country and hasn't put me off contemplating a permanent move out there.

I just have to be a lot more careful ,obviously.

It really has been a remarkable rise from our first days in Stockton Heath. In many ways I can see a certain symmetry to the way this new chapter in our lives has developed and the way my career as a footballer took shape.

The humble, exciting beginnings in Cheshire followed by success on a national and then an international scale. It is fairytale stuff in many ways and I feel so lucky to have enjoyed such highs both on and off the pitch.

Like I say, back when the nurseries first started it was a godsend for me. The thought of watching Liverpool or football in general just didn't appeal. I felt lucky to have something I could really sink my teeth into.

It was a good while before I even contemplated going back to Anfield. I didn't even want to watch matches on Sky Sports. I knew I'd just be sitting there thinking 'I should still be out there.'

I knew it would have just set me back seeing what I was missing out on.

A lot of the former pros do media work but, again, that wasn't for me. I had a few offers to sit on the panels and be a pundit but my interest had waned so much that I just told them that I wouldn't have a clue who played for which team anymore.

Fortunately that's not the case now.

The fact Declan has developed a taste for football and a passion for Liverpool has played a big part in it. I suppose the club is in our genes.

From my granddad right through to Declan now. Whether you play for them or just turn into staunch supporters like Paul, Pete or Declan, it has always played a major role in our family's lives.

A lot of supporters have suggested to me that I could have gone on to play a role in the club's more recent successes had I not had such a tragic run of injuries. Maybe I could have.

If you look at the treble-winning year of 2001, I suppose I would have only been 29. I tend to think I wouldn't have lasted under Houllier anyway and the club also signed Markus Babbel who was a revelation in that right-back role.

It's easy to say if, but and maybe. At the time I felt bitter that my career was over but now I'm just delighted that I had the chance to play for Liverpool and enjoyed a relatively successful career up to that point.

It was only when I started to look back on my football life with that sort of positivity that I was able to recapture my passion for Liverpool FC once again.

CHAPTER THIRTEEN

It's hard to explain the pleasure you get as a father taking your son to his first cup final.

The early morning start, complete with matching Liverpool scarves and a permanent grin. All in expectation of what could turn out to be a day to remember.

Paul had given me my first taste of Wembley when we travelled down for the FA Cup final with Everton back in 1986.

Now I knew how he had felt.

The date was February 2012 and Liverpool were back at Wembley for the first time since I was a player. They'd won a number of trophies at Cardiff's Millennium Stadium whilst the home of English football was being renovated, but since 'new' Wembley reopened in 2007 Liverpool had not been back.

Until now.

I wasn't going to miss it. We had arranged to make a big day of it with Michael Thomas and his son Myan. Ian St John's lad runs a coach service and he had put together a good deal for us. We were picked up at Knutsford services after booking four seats and a table so we could enjoy the trip down to London in style.

It was a great laugh. We were with a bunch of fans and we enjoyed the banter with them. Michael got stick for his title-winning goal for Arsenal and I got the usual about how a few of them had put a pound on me every week to finally get my goal. It was all in good humour.

Thankfully we all came home with big smiles upon our faces too.

Everyone remembers the last time we had been to Wembley. It was back in 1996 with those white suits. That came up in the conversation en route to the capital as well!

Somehow I knew the current crop of players wouldn't be making that mistake ahead of their clash with Championship side Cardiff City.

But there was still the usual rollercoaster of emotions you get as a red.

Falling behind to an early goal, the nervous feeling that it wouldn't be your day, before finally there is the relief of an equaliser.

Then, what looks like being a winning goal in extra-time, prior to a last-gasp leveller that forces penalties.

There's probably a generation of reds out there who think it's par for the course that Liverpool will guarantee a memorable cup final! There also seems to be the obligatory shoot-out that concludes with another piece of silverware making its way to the Anfield trophy cabinet.

Seeing King Kenny parading the Carling Cup with his players meant it really hit home for me how life has come full circle.

Now I was the proud parent watching the reds triumph alongside my son. I was also an avid fan once again.

Gone were the days when the pain of watching Liverpool had been unbearable. Now I was able to enjoy supporting my team from afar.

Everyone loves talking about the miracle of Istanbul and that famous European Cup success of 2005.

I'm no different.

I've heard so many wonderful stories about how fans got there and celebrated the club's fifth triumph in Europe's number one competition.

Alas, mine doesn't come close to gripping the imagination like some of those tales, but I still love recalling it.

I was simply sat alone in my living room with a bottle of red wine as my companion.

The kids were upstairs in bed and I watched on as AC Milan produced a first-half master-class to leave me sinking a few glasses in despair.

What happened in the minutes and hours after the interval is etched in Liverpool's history forever.

I just went mental. I was jumping up and down on the couch screaming. Red wine was flying everywhere, but I didn't care.

A movement out of the corner of my eye caught my attention and I could see the kids huddled together looking at me with a mix of curiosity and bewilderment.

I'm not one for moments of explosive emotion. I'm a quiet, easy going guy who doesn't really get carried away. So it was a relatively new experience for them to see their dad completely lost in the moment like that.

It was a telling evening for me. I'd finally been back to Anfield in the year or so preceding that night, but the rush I experienced as Andriy Shevchenko saw his spot kick saved by Jerzy Dudek took me back to my days singing my heart out on the Kop.

When I think about it now, that stands out as the night my love for Liverpool FC was rekindled. It sums up what the club is all about.

It was like a lightning bolt; a reminder of what the reds mean to me and it proved to be the final piece of the jigsaw in my new life after professional football.

Our business was flourishing and I had started to play for Liverpool's legends. All that had been missing was the fan inside.

Istanbul coupled with my involvement with the legends has been the most significant factor in me falling back in love with the game.

Those trips have become a huge part of my routine and lifestyle.

It's just brilliant to be able to play with players I grew up worshipping, whose careers maybe didn't coincide with mine.

It all began when Phil Neal asked me to go and play in a match the legends were playing in Jamaica.

I was a tad reluctant at first, simply because I was worried the knee wouldn't hold up.

He persisted with the calls and I eventually decided to give it a go.

I'm glad I did.

The banter is fantastic. We get flown all around the world to play prestige matches and are given the superstar treatment.

The matches are 35 minutes each way and the action is not as intense as I had feared. It's more to do with possession, focusing on the old Liverpool adage of letting the ball do the work.

We get a lot of invitations to Scandinavia, Thailand and Singapore. You name it and we've probably been there at some point. There are no shortage of supporters' groups looking to set up a match against a local side.

It's been hugely successful and has almost got to the point where we are flying off somewhere new every other month.

I've even been able to fulfil a big dream of mine from when I was still a teenager.

In the years just prior to my move to Liverpool they had been playing some of the most fantastic football I have ever witnessed. Ian Rush had left for Juventus and we had replaced him with John Aldridge.

I absolutely worshipped Aldo and was gutted that he left. I'd liked to have played in the same Liverpool first-team as him, but it wasn't to be.

Fortunately enough, I got to realise that ambition with the legends. Pulling on the famous red shirt alongside him and enjoying some of his wit is something I'll always remember.

You can go a year without seeing a lot of former reds but as soon as you step on that coach or into that dressing room the banter starts. It's like you have never been away.

Then you have the Christmas meals with the likes of Alan Hansen and Mark Lawrenson involved. It really is great to see all these former reds together and helps to fill the void that is left once you hang up your boots.

My adventures with the legends take up a fair bit of my life nowadays and when I'm not playing in tournaments or discussing business, I tend to spend a lot of my spare time at home.

I'm a bit of a house-husband most days. I take the kids to school and pick them up. Sue is the business tycoon of the family!

I did run a soccer school in Ellesmere Port with Danny Murphy's brother for four years or so, but in the end it wasn't what I hoped it would be. It felt like more of a child-minding service than a place to hone their skills. Parents were dropping disinterested kids off for the day so they could have a break in the school holidays.

Some of them didn't want to learn what you were trying to teach them and that became hugely frustrating. I got bored of it and quit.

That was it for my involvement with football coaching until the day Declan started showing an interest. Straight away you could see he had a nice touch and good awareness. I had to laugh to myself. 'Here we go again,' I thought.

He loves football and is an avid red. Of course, his dad wouldn't let him dream of being anything else!

He had a few sessions at Crewe when he was eight and I used to take him down to their Academy. Naturally, Dario was there and it was great to bump into a few faces I hadn't seen in such a long time.

To be honest, all I wanted was to see how he got on. He hasn't been for a while now. Too much focus is on players being big and strong physically, even at that age.

His coach insisted he didn't go anywhere else because he could see he has something about him as a player. He didn't want me taking him over to Liverpool.

Funnily enough, I bumped into their Academy director, Frank McParland not so long ago and he was asking me what Declan was like.

He said he'd be interested in having a look at him. I left it open because I didn't want to commit.

I just want Declan to enjoy it because he's still young. If it goes anywhere then great. If not, there certainly won't be any pressure from myself or Sue.

If he did have what it takes to carve out a career in the game then we will be there to support him all of the way. I may well end up taking him back to Crewe. After all, it didn't do me any harm and you see too many kids with potential not given a chance at the big clubs. You don't have the opportunity to grow as a player if you are playing reserve team football into your 20s.

Just like any kid, his dream is to play for Liverpool. As I have mentioned, I took him to Melwood not so long ago after arranging a surprise visit courtesy of the kindness of Jamie Carragher.

He made a big fuss of Declan and introduced him to Steven Gerrard. I was aware of Steven when he was coming through the ranks but didn't really cross paths with him at first-team level. He was great with both Declan and myself.

Declan was buzzing after that and I've seen him recreating some of Steven's goals in the back yard from time to time. I wonder where he gets that from?

I don't know what his destiny holds but nothing would give me greater pride than to see him become the next generation of the Jones clan to run out at Anfield and wear the liverbird upon his chest.

Having said that, there's no expectation or hope on our part. We just want him to be happy.

But who knows... maybe it's in his blood.

THE END.

LEGENDS PAY TRIBUTE TO ROB JONES

It says a great deal about Rob Jones the man as much as it does about Rob Jones the footballer that ex-managers, teammates and even fierce opponents were keen to offer their views on why they regard him as one of the finest right-backs this country has ever produced.

From Ryan Giggs and Dario Gradi through to Jamie Carragher and Graeme Souness, the next few pages provide a glowing eulogy of a talent cruelly cut short by injury.

JAMIE CARRAGHER

Liverpool's second all-time appearance holder Jamie Carragher explains why Rob Jones should have gone on to make his own mark on the standings of the players who have featured most for English football's most successful club.

It's a cold February night in Teesside and Jamie Carragher can feel his heart skip a beat as the call comes for him to get stripped and ready.

It's the 75th minute of a League Cup tie at the Riverside and former England right back Rob Jones is the player who Roy Evans opts to replace, as Bootle-born Carra comes on to make his Reds debut.

Jones would go on to play just 28 more times for Liverpool as injuries finally put paid to what had promised to be an outstanding Anfield career.

Carra on the other hand has now played over 700 matches for the Reds and is the club's second highest appearance holder ever.

So what does Liverpool's current vice-captain recall about the man whose injury problems opened the door for him to make his first mark upon the first-team set-up?

"I was still a young lad hoping to make the grade when Rob Jones was at his best," says Carragher in an exclusive interview for this book.

"He was an outstanding full-back. He had pace, awareness, he could get forward and rarely let his man past him.

"I remember chatting with him on the team coach around the time I first got called into the squad. He was a really good guy. To be honest, there's not much to tell in terms of banter or funny anecdotes because I was at the stage where I was just starting to get in the squad and I wasn't about to jump up and make jokes.

"In a strange way we were both in a similar position. Obviously I was much younger but we were both trying to get a run of games in the side. He was just coming back from the injury that he had picked up just after the 1996 FA Cup final and I was looking to show Roy Evans what I could do.

"I've played at right back myself, particularly when I first started to get a real run of games in the side and it was probably his injury problems that gave me some opportunities.

"It says much about his quality as a full-back that he was able to switch to left-wing back when Jason McAteer arrived and comfortably adapt to the position. Again, I've played that role and know how hard it is when it isn't your favoured side.

"When you look back at the best Liverpool full-backs of all-time – not just right backs – Rob Jones has to be up there.

"Sadly injury halted what could have been a glittering career. Who knows what would have happened? I don't think the club would have needed to have signed anyone for that position in the years that followed because he would have held it himself.

"We brought in Vegard Heggem and Markus Babbel and the latter went on to have a massive impact on the treble-winning season. He was a great player for us but if Rob had been fit, the manager would not have been looking for a right-back.

"Most supporters would point to Phil Neal as the club's best right-back ever because of the medals that he won and the crucial goals he scored in European finals.

"If Rob had stayed fit he could well have been part of the treble-winning team and maybe even Istanbul. Then he'd have the medals to go with his outstanding performances and he'd be on a par with the Phil Neal's of this world.

"I suppose it just wasn't to be for him. Some players are simply unlucky with injury. It's a sad part of the game. I'm one of the ones who has been relatively fortunate with injuries. Yes, I've broken my leg and more recently dislocated my shoulder, but generally I've been okay and have managed to play a lot of games for this club.

"There's no doubt in anyone's mind that Rob could have added far more to the number of matches he played here.

"We only really played the one season in the same squad back in 1997-98. Even then it seemed that when he was in the side I wouldn't be and vice versa.

"I do remember a Merseyside derby we played together. Duncan Ferguson gave Everton the lead at Anfield before Paul Ince equalised for us.

"I think I was at centre back that day with Steve Harkness. He was on the left and Bjorn Tore Kvarme on the right. I suppose that wasn't the strongest of back fours was it?

"I was always amazed that he didn't get his goal for Liverpool. He was such an attacking full-back and always got into great positions. It just wouldn't go in for him.

"I also know what it's like not to trouble the score sheet very often but it is a real thrill to score for Liverpool and I'm sure he'd loved to have done it. Having said that, I'd rather have a full-back that defends well, covers for his centre backs and can also support the attack when needed. He did all these things and more.

"When I think back to his best games I suppose I'll be like everyone else and pick out his first-team debut for Liverpool. Coming from Crewe like that and playing against Manchester United at Old Trafford was a daunting task. He handled Ryan Giggs well and you knew then Liverpool had unearthed a player.

"He had a superb England debut against France too. Martin Keown and Alan Shearer also made their international bows but much of the talk after the match was about Rob.

"People make out that Gerard Houllier looked to get rid of players from that so-called era of the 'spice boys'. Personally, I don't think that's fair because all Gerard was looking to do was keep players he felt had the right attitude to play for the club and remove those he felt didn't.

"I don't think Rob came into this because he wasn't really part of that side of things. So, like I said, I think a fully fit Rob Jones would have been a fixture in Gerard's team. It was only because of his lengthy absences through injury that Liverpool looked to other players to fill the position.

"I think Gary Neville would have had a real job on his hands to have kept hold of the England right-back jersey if Rob had been injury-free too. That's no disrespect to Gary because he's enjoyed great success in the game and was a great servant for England.

"But Rob was an all-round better full-back – I suppose I'm always going to say that though aren't I!

"It's a shame he missed out on Euro 92 and Euro 96 because I think he was a player that had the quality to excel at that level.

"He could easily have gone down as the best right-back in Europe during that era and I'd have loved to have played a lot more matches with him."

RYAN GIGGS

There are few rivalries as fierce as Liverpool and Manchester United.

It is a clash that transcends the source of its North-West roots to enthral and ignite the passion of a global audience.

It was on one such occasion, back in 1991, that Rob Jones made the first of his 243 appearances for the Merseyside outfit at Old Trafford.

Such was the calibre of his performance it prompted Ryan Giggs, United's latest prodigy and now their most decorated player, to describe Jones as the best opponent he had ever faced in an interview some years later.

Since those early battles Giggs has gone on to achieve unparalleled success with the Red Devils, claiming no fewer than 12 league title winners' medals, two Champions Leagues and four FA Cup triumphs.

In a career now stretching into its third decade he has come up against some of the greatest full-backs ever seen; so to assert that Rob Jones remains the finest exponent of the full-back art he has gone head-to-head with would be perhaps too much to expect, wouldn't it?

"Well, it was many, many years ago and very early in my senior career, but nevertheless I stand by what I said at the time," said Giggs in an exclusive interview for this book.

"Rob, like me, was in the fledgling days of his career at the top level and he proved to be a very difficult opponent. I have faced some of the World's finest full-backs over the years, but I still remember Rob as one of the most formidable defenders.

"I think that it goes without saying that I felt for him when I heard he had to retire at such an early age. It is always a tragedy when a player is forced to quit through injury. Nobody in the game takes any pleasure from seeing a player's time at the top cut short.

"Rob was enjoying an excellent career before suffering knee problems. What happened to him does make me hugely thankful that in the main I escaped the type of injuries that denied him a longer period as a professional.

"He was an extremely accomplished defender who didn't need to be asked twice to join the attack. He was a modern full-back in every sense of the word and was amongst the very best until his playing days were curtailed."

From Cafu and Lilian Thuram through to the likes of Daniel Alves - there are no shortage of contenders for the role of 'toughest ever opponent' for Giggs to mull over when he does eventually hang up his boots.

It's the type of question a player is asked repeatedly over the years. Whilst some find it rather tiresome, it often elicits a response that causes great debate amongst fans.

Not that Giggs is willing to reveal all just yet.

"I'm not going to list the best or worst full-backs I have ever faced because some of them are still playing," he said.

"But the fact that Rob occupies a prominent place in Liverpool's all-time favourites confirms that my initial impression of his ability wasn't far from the mark.

"Let's be honest, you've got to pretty handy to establish yourself in Liverpool's first team and Rob played enough times to become a real favourite with the Anfield crowd. There can be little doubt that he's one of Liverpool's best defenders during the Premier League era and it's really sad that injury had to halt his career when it was nearing its peak."

Having racked up over 900 appearances for Manchester United and compiled his own A-Z of high profile encounters, it would be easy for Giggs to have forgotten the moment he first locked horns with Jones.

After all it was hardly a classic was it?

"I do remember the game. A 0-0 draw back in October 1991 at Old Trafford. I also recall being impressed with this young lad from Crewe that everyone was talking about before kick off," said Giggs.

"He fitted seamlessly into their defence and gave a performance that must have had the Liverpool bench smiling from ear to ear.

"I was asked if I'd ever heard of him after the match, but his display hadn't surprised me. Crewe Alexandra is famous throughout football for producing fine young players and word always gets around about the latest youngsters on the Gresty Road conveyor belt. We've recently signed Nick Powell from them so they are still doing it now.

"I remember Rob was being tipped for a big future before he was transferred to Anfield and that display was proof they had done some good business in signing him.

"We had a few great battles in the years that followed. I'm sure we had our moments but I don't remember anything more than the usual banter that goes on in every match. I cannot imagine there has ever been a United v Liverpool game where the odd exchange of views hasn't taken place. Rob was an excellent defender, but I like to think that I gave as good as I got too."

Jones continued to ride the crest of a wave in the weeks and months that followed that first Old Trafford showdown, and it appeared that a glittering international career was beckoning when he made his full England bow just after the turn of the year.

However, a series of troublesome injuries coupled with Gary Neville's emergence at Manchester United meant he would go on to play just eight times for his country while the Red Devils' right-back clocked up 85 caps.

Giggs makes no secret of the fact he has great admiration for his former teammate but concedes that the Sky Sports pundit would have had a greater task to hold down his place had Jones remained fully fit.

"Not surprisingly, I rate Gary Neville very highly," he said.

"He was a far better player than he was viewed in some quarters and a fantastic servant to both Manchester United and England. But there can be little doubt that Rob would have presented him with stiff competition for that right-back berth.

"Of course, having first seen the light of day in Wrexham, he should have played for Wales! Then we could have been teammates for years!"

It 's obvious that Giggs has huge respect for the performances Rob Jones produced both against him and during his entire career as a Premier League footballer.

The United star is himself one of the modern era's greatest ever players and yet his humility is remarkable given his tremendous success.

When told that Jones regards him as the toughest opponent he ever faced, his response is genuine and grounded.

"You cannot receive a bigger compliment than one delivered by a fellow professional, but it is still enormously flattering," he said.

"There can be few bigger rivalries in football than the one which exists between Manchester United and Liverpool, but the players of each club have the greatest respect for each other and it says a lot that we are happy to readily acknowledge the strengths of our opponents.

"I have an enormous amount of time for someone like Rob and will always remember him as a great adversary."

DARIO GRADI

Crewe Alexandra's reputation as a hot-bed of young talent has not waned throughout their long association with Dario Gradi.

The man is undoubtedly the most iconic figure in the Railwaymen's history and remains a significant influence on the League One outfit to this day.

Back in 1988 the former Surrey school teacher sold David Platt to Aston Villa for a fee of £200,000 and most recently, Crewe secured £3 million from Manchester United for the services of the highly-rated Nick Powell.

The fact they were able to command such a figure is evidence of the respect they have earned as a breeding ground for the rough diamonds of English football.

According to Gradi, it is a lucrative process that was kick-started by Rob Jones's move to Liverpool.

Not a high-flyer.

Those were the words that sprung to mind when I first came across Rob Jones.

He was only a young lad at the time and I have to be honest - he wasn't outstanding. I felt he had some decent attributes; such as good technique, a strong temperament and when I spoke with him afterwards it was clear he was a nice kid.

We decided to take a chance and get him into our youth set-up to see how he developed. I'm pleased to say we weren't disappointed.

At the age of 15 he grew noticeably quicker, to the point where he had blistering pace. In short, I believe that was what made him into a player.

It was that lightning speed that made it an easy decision for me to convert him into a full-back. He was that quick that no-one was going to get beyond him.

That pace seemed to raise his confidence and he became what I term a 'high-flyer'. Danny Murphy was a 'high-flyer' from day one but that wasn't the case with Rob. He grew into one.

It was after one particular cup game that I knew he was ready for the topflight.

He'd played against a team in a higher league and he was simply outstanding.

We'd had enquiries from clubs about him, but not what I would call a 'big' club. I wasn't willing to let him go unless they were going to put him in the first-team. Nowadays we can't do that because the standard and gap in quality has changed so much.

I couldn't say to Manchester United that we aren't going to sell you Nick Powell because they won't put him in the first team straight away, especially when they are going to pay us £3million.

I remember Brian Clough enquired about Rob at Nottingham Forest, but they weren't going to put him in the team.

We had quite a good relationship with Liverpool and they said to us that they were looking for a full-back. They asked if we could recommend someone in the league. I didn't suggest Rob because I didn't think he would be capable of going into Liverpool's team. However, after the game in question, I decided that he could.

So I rang them up and said that we did have someone who was playing left-back for us, but he was even better at right-back.

I quite like having wide players who can cut in on their good foot and Rob was more than capable of doing that on the left.

Anyway, they came and had a look and told us they wanted to buy him. They actually said to us that we had the best right-back in the lower leagues and I was crazy to be playing him on the left.

I was aware of that and asked the question; was he going to play in the first-team? I got the response I wanted and more. I was told that he would indeed and that it was highly likely he would be playing against Manchester United on Sunday, marking Ryan Giggs.

It was a remarkable rise. Rob had broken into our first-team at quite a young age and I'd say he was holding his own at first. But as he grew in confidence, he suddenly developed into a terrific player. In my mind that happened quite quickly and after that he made that step up into the topflight seamlessly.

I regard him as our first really big transfer.

David Platt went for £200,000 which was an astronomical fee. No-one anticipated we would blow that out of the water with Rob.

I was called into a board meeting just after Liverpool's contact. I told them I'd sold Rob Jones for around half a million pounds. I think if I had told them then that I wanted a 20-year contract they'd have given it to me on the spot!

It was very good money at the time. For me, it set the standard for selling players at Crewe.

We recently sold Powell to Man United and we decided that we wanted £3million for him. That's not easy when you consider what division we are in. The fee could rise to six in years to come.

The point is that teams expect to pay good money for our best players and Rob set that standard. It was great for everyone involved because he settled straight in at Liverpool and went on to play for England within six months. It was fairytale stuff.

He actually came and trained with us with a view to making a comeback a few years after he hung up his boots. But the insurance company would have wanted their money back after paying out for his early retirement. There was no guarantee that his knee would stand up to it either, so after weighing it all up he decided against it.

I tried to convince him to come back to Crewe as a coach instead, but he politely declined. I don't think he fancied it. He's got a great life now with a fantastic nursery business, not to mention the fact he flies all around the world playing with Liverpool's legends.

He is most definitely amongst the best players to have ever come through Crewe's system.

I couldn't possibly say if he was THE best because we've unearthed a lot of talent over the years.

They all give me satisfaction in different ways.

I have a great deal of admiration for Rob as a player and as a person.

I've coached some fine players at different levels during my time involved in the game and if I was picking my all-time XI, he would most certainly have a place in my team.

And there's no doubt in my mind that he'd be a 'high-flyer' in that side.

GRAEME SOUNESS

By his own admission, some of Graeme Souness's signings as Liverpool manager didn't quite live up to expectations.

The Scot spent big money on numerous occasions during his brief time in the Anfield dugout, but was rarely repaid with the type of performances befitting what he believes is necessary of a Liverpool player.

Rob Jones was a notable exception.

The young full-back represented something of a gamble for the former Rangers boss, one that he was delighted to see pay off.

Here he explains how he came to sign the Crewe defender and why he feels one of his finest recruits should have been an Anfield great.

I can remember quite vividly the night that I first saw Rob Jones in action.

I went to see Crewe play at Gresty Road and I took my seat in the directors' box alongside Tom Saunders.

We'd heard about a young full-back who could have what it takes to make the step up and I was interested to see what he had to offer.

Tom had worked closely with Bob Paisley and Joe Fagan and was a man widely credited with playing a key role in bringing in some of the best players Liverpool have ever had.

On this occasion, it didn't take long for us to realise we had a player on our hands.

Right away I felt Rob was the stand out performer. He was extremely athletic and very quick. For someone who was so young, he also showed great confidence.

I looked towards Tom midway through the action and I could tell by his expression he was thinking the same thing. Rob was worth taking a chance on. We knew Crewe didn't want a lot of money, so I decided to act.

I spoke with Peter Robinson, with whom I had a great relationship and he got in touch with the relevant people at Crewe. I think we paid £300,000 initially, rising to over half a million with appearances.

We got him in ahead of a massive game against Manchester United at Old Trafford and I put him straight into training with the first-team to see how he got on.

He wasn't overawed in any way, shape or form. He didn't look out of place and the comments the coaching staff made to me afterwards were glowing. They said that he looked like he had been with us for years.

He'd gone from a comparatively low standard at Crewe to playing with some really talented players at Liverpool in a matter of days, and he dealt with it all very well. He took it all in his stride. You have to understand that the speed and way players move the ball at the top level is very different. Those who come up from other divisions take time to adjust. In some cases, they never get used to it. However, Rob settled right away, which is a big compliment to him.

I was so impressed that I decided to throw him straight in. I know a lot of people questioned that. I figured that he had handled the training with no problem and I was interested to see how he would deal with the big stage. They don't come any bigger than Old Trafford. He had around 45,000 people screaming at him and they all knew he was a novice.

Many would have frozen under the spotlight. But not him.

I think his personality helped. I kept an eye on him in the dressing room before kick off and he looked so calm. He wasn't over-excited and didn't appear too anxious.

It just all went over his head and that's what I recall about that day. The way he coped with the entire occasion. He had an excellent debut on a ground that is arguably the hardest place for Liverpool to go to.

He was a very popular lad. That spoke volumes for him because he was coming from a different world in Crewe. The banter of our dressing room can be tough for someone who isn't a Liverpool-type of player, but he dealt with it with ease. Yes, he was the butt of the jokes at that point, but he handled that in his own way and he quickly grasped what it was all about playing for that club. You sink or swim. He was determined to swim and he certainly did that.

He went up against Ryan Giggs and he didn't give him a kick. He had electric pace and was confident on the ball for someone so inexperienced.

We thought we had bought someone for the future, but he turned out to be for the present. That was a tremendous bonus for us.

He never really realised the full potential of his career because of his back and knee injuries. He was someone who had natural athleticism and I think he is the type of player who would have gone on to play for a long, long time, well into his 30s.

The injuries were all that stopped him from being classed as a truly great player.

For me, greatness doesn't just come from being a stand out performer, it comes from playing at the highest level for a long period of time.

In terms of ability he was certainly as good as Phil Neal, a man regarded as the best right-back Liverpool have ever had.

Don't forget, I played with Phil and I can tell you he was an excellent footballer. But I think Rob had more pace and matched Phil for the never-say-die spirit and desire not to be beaten by his man. Having said that, I think you have to put Nealy in front of him.

When you look at the number of medals Phil has got it shows that he was a mainstay in an outstanding team. Rob may not come close to matching that but when you are just talking about pure ability, then he is up there with the Phil Neals of this world.

He should also have won countless caps for his country. Whether he was up against Lee Dixon, Paul Parker or Gary Neville, I think Rob shaded them all when it came to the overall ability of a full back.

Without a doubt he was one of the best, if not the best, signing I made as Liverpool manager.

It was obviously a personal tragedy for him that his career was cut short by injury but I think it was also sad for Liverpool. He should have been a 15-year man for the club because, like I say, he was good enough to do that.

Not many are.

NOTES

NOTES